Barbara Hill has practised graphology for the past twelve years. She is particularly interested in using handwriting analysis to help disturbed children and as an aid in careers guidance. Educated at Dorking County Grammar School and the Kingston School of Art, she is married to the painter and illustrator Geoffrey Bargery. They have two teenaged sons.

Handwriting Analysis

BARBARA HILL

Hamlyn Paperbacks

HANDWRITING ANALYSIS
ISBN 0 600 20774 9

First published in Great Britain 1981
by Robert Hale Limited under the title *Graphology*
Hamlyn Paperbacks edition 1983
Copyright © 1981 by Barbara Hill

Hamlyn Paperbacks are published by
The Hamlyn Publishing Group Ltd,
Astronaut House, Feltham,
Middlesex, England

Printed and bound in Great Britain by
Cox & Wyman Ltd, Reading

For my mother

Contents

Contents

Introduction

The definition of graphology is 'estimating character from handwriting' (Greek: graphe, a writing; logos, discourse).

Character consists of observable behaviour (which is objective), expressed inner experience (which is subjective) and conscious and unconscious behaviour-response patterns (which include adaptation to environment and human relationships). It reflects the nature of a person's psychological defence system (his ability to adapt himself to external circumstances and his ability to arrange external circumstances to suit himself) and ego defences (which are automatic stabilizers of the mind). Character, therefore, is a compromise between inner and outer forces: it is the result of an evaluation of the claims of the ego and the demands of reality.

To be conversant with the ramifications of character, the graphologist must have a basic knowledge of psychology, psychiatry, pathology, physiology, sexology and sociological criminology. He must have an extensive education, a comprehension of social and cultural strata, self-discipline, insight and empathy.

The term 'scientific graphology', which is frequently used nowadays, is, in fact, a misnomer. 'Scientific' implies accuracy. Graphology is never accurate because a balanced assessment relies entirely on the ability of the individual analyst to observe objectively and to evaluate subjectively the graphological features in a handwriting. Graphology is an art to which is applied the knowledge of various sciences and a well-equipped graphologist can achieve a high degree of reliable character interpretation.

The graphologist must not be confused with the hand-writing expert; the graphologist is concerned with the character of a person, the handwriting expert with the physical structure of a handwriting.

A Short History of Graphology

As far as is known, the first book about graphology was written by an Italian doctor and published in Capri in 1622. Subsequently, several articles were published in Italy, France and Switzerland up to the 1800s. In 1823, Stephen Collett, an Englishman, published a book relating character to handwriting.

Modern graphology is associated with Jean Michon, a Frenchman, who coined the term 'graphology' and who spent years studying, at first hand, the characters and handwritings of thousands of people. He began to publish his findings in 1872. In 1895, in Germany, Wilhelm Langenbruch founded a graphological periodical and in 1897 Hans Busse founded not only another magazine but also a society for graphological research. One of the contri-butors to his magazine was Dr Ludwig Klages whose achievements in graphological research were renowned. Dr Klages later moved to Switzerland where he devised a system of analysis based on standards of handwriting. Using Dr Klage's theories as a basis, Robert Saudek, a Czechoslovakian, concerned himself with the differences between the copybook writings of different countries. He made a special study of English handwriting.

Max Pulver, from Switzerland, was interested in symbols found in handwriting; Hans Jacoby paralleled marks in handwriting with body gestures and I and many other people have done research and made specialised studies in the various fields of human nature.

1 Writing

A child will instinctively choose to use either his right hand or his left hand. It is generally accepted that, in a right-handed child (who will be right-eyed and right-footed as well) the motor impulse relates to a corresponding physiological pattern in the left cerebral hemisphere and that, in a left-handed child (who will be left-eyed and left-footed) the motor impulse relates to a corresponding physiological pattern in the right cerebral hemisphere. Therefore, if the left-handed child is made to write with his right hand, the disruption of the relationship between the left motor impulse and right physiological pattern will cause intellectual difficulties in learning, speech and so on.

The act of writing is an unconscious response to brain impulses which stimulate the flexor and extensor muscles of the forearm to contract and extend the fingers. The written word is important as a means of communication, establishing contact, understanding and relationships between people but, although the need for legibility is obvious, we all write differently in varying degrees of legibility and illegibility according to our unconscious response to brain impulse.

Any movement is caused by brain impulse. As a gesture of the head, arm or leg reveals an attitude of mind so, too, does the act of handwriting. In fact, we write very much in the way that we speak and move. A person who speaks rapidly will walk quickly and will write with speed. A person who speaks slowly and clearly will walk with dignity and will write carefully. A person who speaks loudly and colourfully will walk jauntily and will write with a flamboyant hand. A person who stutters may well walk with a pronounced lack of grace and write with jerky, hesitating movements.

2   Children

A young child's scribbling gives a spontaneous, graphic account of his response to the world around him. For example, a wide, open scribble shows happiness; a cramped scribble reveals anxiety; a scribble that grows smaller on a downward slope indicates dejection; a scribble consisting of heavy, violent strokes personifies rage. The marks the child makes will create a pattern which so satisfies him he will repeat it time and again. This repetitive pattern becomes his own familiar form of individual expression and will appear in his handwriting throughout his life, most noticeably in connective forms, stroke endings and flourishes on the signature.

Fig. 1 shows an angular scribble which has been done very quickly with heavy pressure but is well connected, controlled and regular. It was drawn by a child who is confident, extravert, determined and brave: his natural independence allows him to mix easily with other children. Fig. 2 was drawn by a happy, gentle child: the light, curving pattern reveals generosity and a powerful imagination. One can almost feel the concentrated effort needed to draw the confused and irregular pattern in Fig. 3. The chaotic areas reveal intense agitation and the constricted strokes, inhibition: the child is unconsciously suppressing instinctual impulses, and releases his frustration in aggressive outbursts. A pattern without cohesion but drawn with original and sensitive lines, as in Fig. 4, is the work of a timid but gifted child who needs firm encouragement to express himself in constructive ways.

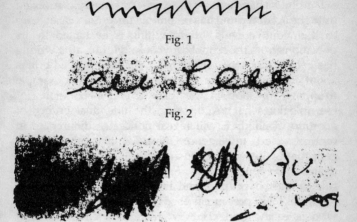

Fig. 1

Fig. 2

Fig. 3   Fig. 4

An effective test of a child's intelligence, based on his drawing of a human figure, was devised by Florence Goodenough in 1926. Any child under the age of six years who spontaneously makes graphic *constructions* is illustrating his intelligence and it is generally accepted that a young child who spontaneously draws a triangle with all angles precisely joined is revealing a high degree of mental development.

When a child goes to school and learns to write the alphabet he finds that he must suppress his own spontaneous familiar markings and follow an obligatory copybook pattern. It is a fact, however, that a child's suppressed individual expression will find an escape route; this usually takes the form of embellishments or the underlining of letters to which he has an unconscious emotional attachment. A group of children who painstakingly copy an obligatory pattern will all produce different results because their individual expressiveness will unconsciously colour their efforts.

In a child's handwriting the character is not fully revealed until the act of writing has become an unconscious habit; up to this point a child's handwriting is evaluated by its deviations from the school copybook style but, after writing has become an unconscious habit, increased speed brings about modifications such as simplification (for example dropping the loop of the letter l) and elaboration (for example flourishes). At this stage the individual writings of a group of children will reveal noticeable differences in maturity and intelligence. Neat writing and careful punctuation reveal a good memory, co-operation and a desire to be conscientious. Regular, heavy pressure indicates a sense of purpose and a natural mental and physical strength. Light pressure is used by the impressionable child who is easily influenced by his surroundings. Upright handwriting points to the child who prefers to be by himself—the bookworm or the enthusiastic model-maker.

Poor handwriting should never be corrected by force for it could indicate an emotional disturbance or a disorder in development. If a child finds great difficulty in producing a good handwriting he should be encouraged to use a soft lead pencil (2B or BB) or felt-tip pens: a smoother, easier action will inspire confidence. Consistently poor hand-writing should always be investigated; such an obvious lack of co-operation is usually caused by a disturbance in the child. The retrospective study of a child's handwriting will reveal when the disturbance began and an analysis of events at that time may well disclose the root cause of the child's dissatisfaction. When emotional balance is restored the child's handwriting will improve.

3   Puberty

As puberty develops the personality changes. Sex characteristics and erotic feelings come up against the discipline of society causing a certain amount of confusion, emotionalism and aggression. There is often found in handwriting, at this stage, sudden bursts of pressure (uncontrollable expression), exaggeration of size (combating inferiority), a left slant—especially in girls' writing (emotional reactions) or extreme left slant (defiance or withdrawal). The idea of independence is taking root and parental authority becomes a hindrance: rebellion, as a consequence, is normal and is graphically illustrated by many oddities appearing within the handwriting (huge loops, changes in slant direction, blotches, uneven pressure).

Hero-worship is common and handwriting may suddenly take the form of imitation expressing an unconscious identification with the hero.

4 Adolescence

Adolescence, the period of youth from puberty to maturity (roughly between the ages of 12 and 20 years) is a time of indecision (t bars do not go through the stem), slack behaviour, nihilistic attitudes and a proneness to accidents (weak pressure). Generally, around the seventeenth year, adolescents will assert their independence (stronger pressure, stable lines, larger capitals), replacing narcissistic feelings with tuism and developing object relationships which will naturally lead to the adult stage and full maturity.

5 Legibility

The faster we write the less legible the writing. Legible writing, therefore, is fairly slow writing (Fig. 5). The person who writes legibly is desiring to be understood; he is an honest and reliable type but lacks impulse or any individual expression. Legibility in a cultured handwriting, with good distances between words and lines, reveals the ability to speak lucidly. Exaggerated legibility, where perfectly legible words are underlined many times (Fig. 6), is the result of the writer's almost paranoiac wish to make himself absolutely clear: he lacks the qualities for social adaptation, i.e. comprehension, discrimination, foresight, method, reasoning. In Fig. 7 the words are legible enough to be read as 'very nearly' but the writer has been lax in the construction of the individual letters, reducing them to casual shapes. He is reflecting his attitude to life: he avoids what is to him the severity of reality by creating agreeable fantasies in which to lose himself.

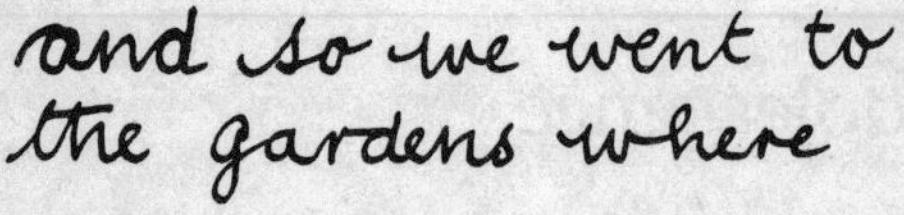

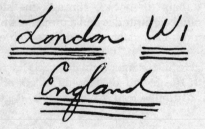

Fig. 5

Fig. 6

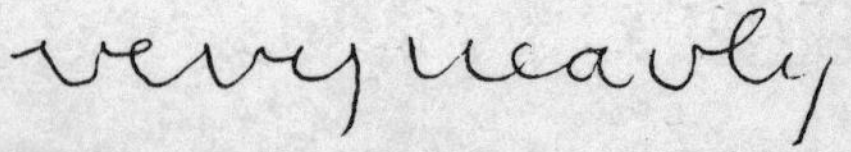

Fig. 7

6   Illegibility

The person who writes illegibly does not wish to be easily understood: he is reluctant to communicate. Some people are so reserved or ineffectual that the demands of everyday living cause them to become withdrawn, obstinate or unadaptable. Others, for various reasons, are so beset by guilt that, in writing, as in speaking, when touching on dangerous or embarrassing grounds, their words become confused: both writing and speaking become indistinct.

Illegibility reveals inferiority, irritation and lack of discipline. An effort to overcome inferiority can be seen in Fig. 8: inferiority compels constant self-observation and the writer has touched-up letters with the intention of making them easier to read but, instead, his neurosis has caused illegibility. An irritated state of mind (characteristic of a traumatic neurosis) is the cause of irrational and inconsiderate behaviour: it is reflected in Fig. 9 where movement is irregular, spatial arrangement is poor and the word 'London' is rendered illegible.

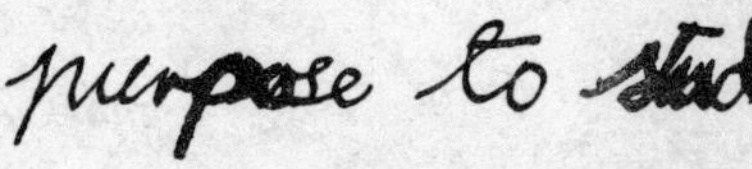

Fig. 8

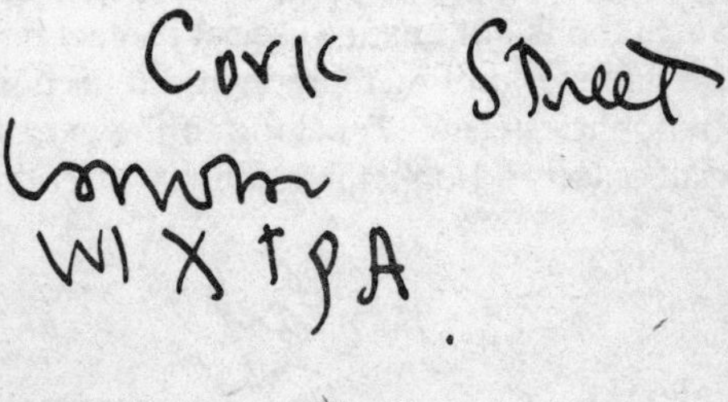

Fig. 9

7 Omissions

Omissions are common to everyone's handwriting. Haste, lack of concentration or a sudden interruption can all cause the leaving out of a word-ending or the failure to cross a t. Frequent omissions, however, point to the writer being in a greatly irritated state of mind. Omissions of upstrokes, or parts of upstrokes, giving the writing a fragmented appearance as in Fig. 10, is indicative of impaired speech or difficulty in articulation. It could also represent an obsession which, as an idea, emotion or impulse, repetitively and insistently forces itself into the writer's unconsciousness creating fatigue in the thinking process and, therefore, weakness in the extensor muscle response.

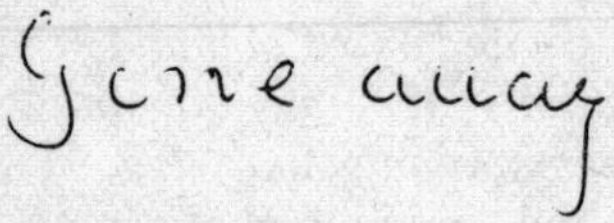

Fig. 10

8 Direction

The direction of the endings of letters are indicative of temperament. Left-direction tendencies (Fig. 11) suggest the introvert who is not given to social contact but prefers his own private world of meditation and reflection. Right-direction tendencies (Fig. 12) belong to the extravert who enjoys social contact and looks to the future with enthusiasm.

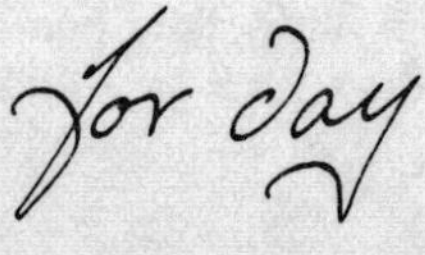

Fig. 11

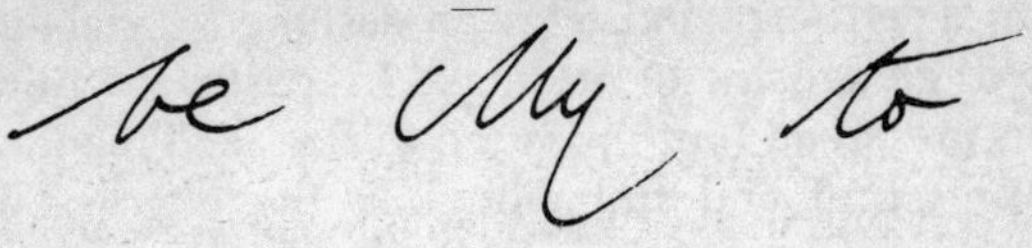

Fig. 12

9 Pressure

Pressure is detected in the difference between upstrokes and downstrokes and between downstrokes and side-strokes. (Evidence of the force of pressure can be seen on the reverse side of a sheet of writing.) Pressure is caused by muscular tension of the fingers in response to brain impulse; pressure, therefore, reflects individual expression. As in speech, when words of strong feeling unconsciously assume a tone of intensity thus revealing aroused emotions so, too, in writing areas of emotional content are revealed by unconscious emphasis of pressure. Unusually heavy pressure at the beginning of a piece of writing, however, is the result of self-consciousness.

There are varying degrees of pressure. *Very light* pressure is the mark of extreme sensitivity. The writer of Fig. 13 is a gentle, kind person who is of a timid disposition and is easily discouraged: lack of energy and an almost constant state of tiredness cause periods of touchiness but never aggression. *Light* pressure (Fig. 14) reveals a quiet, cultured, retiring personality; softly spoken and unassuming but alert and active with a flexible, receptive mind. People writing with light pressure usually choose a smooth-surfaced paper which allows the pen to move easily and freely, caressing rather than assaulting the paper. Very large writing with light pressure (Fig. 15) reveals a casual, undisciplined manner. Tall, wide letters with light pressure and a right slant suggest impatience and lack of concentration; a left slant indicates an assumed sociability and affected generosity of feelings. In pastose writing the strokes are broad (but produced in a relaxed manner with little pressure) and full with ink: the effect is warm, sensuous and colourful (Fig. 16). People who write in this way are physical types indulging wholeheartedly in the pleasures of Nature—lovemaking, food, rich colour, the land. Pastose with a left slant indicates that the writer derives his pleasure from inanimate objects such as architecture or sculpture. *Heavy pressure* expresses primitive elements—energy, ardour, persistence, tenacity, resistance. Combined with speed (Fig. 17) it reveals a considerable energy force: the writer attacks work and play alike with the vitality of a whirlwind. Where all downstrokes only are in heavy pressure (Fig. 18) we find the egoist whose self-centredness and ultra-ambitions compensate for sexual inhibition. Regular heavy pressure on the last downstroke of words or sentences (Fig. 19) indicate dictatorial attitudes. Lassitude and apathy are reflected in 'valleys' (Fig. 20) which are caused by heavy pressure and slight halts at the turning points of strokes.

Pressure may be emphasized horizontally instead of vertically when the sexual libido is transferred from its habitual instinctual area to that of conscious activities. A satisfactory substitutional outlet for sexual expression will be evident from undisturbed writing. Disturbed writing reveals frustration and tension (Fig. 21).

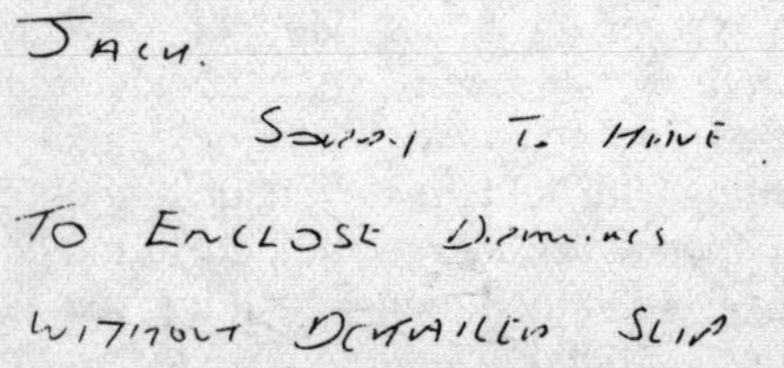

Fig. 13

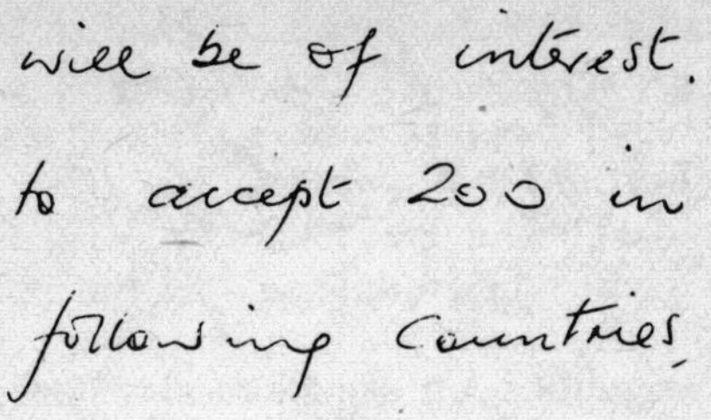

will be of interest.

to accept 200 in

following countries,

Fig. 14

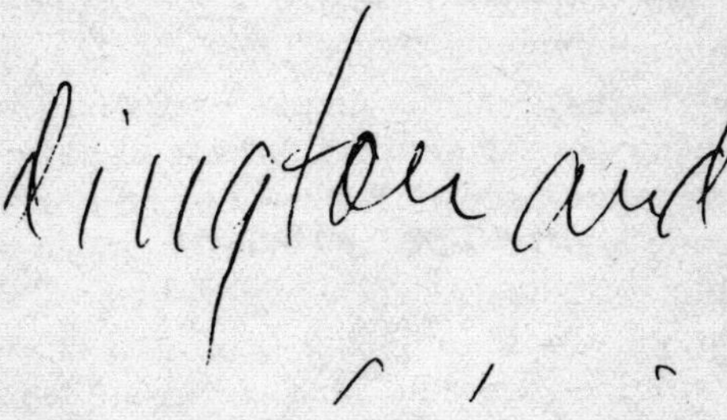

dillgton and

Fig. 15

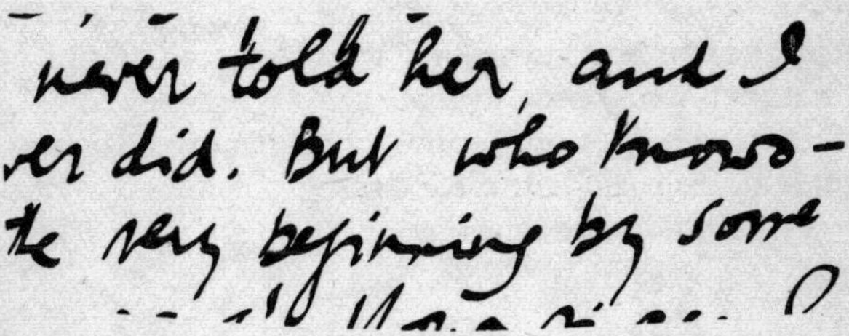

never told her, and I
ver did. But who knows —
the very beginning by some

Fig. 16

'ter Bochua

Fig. 17

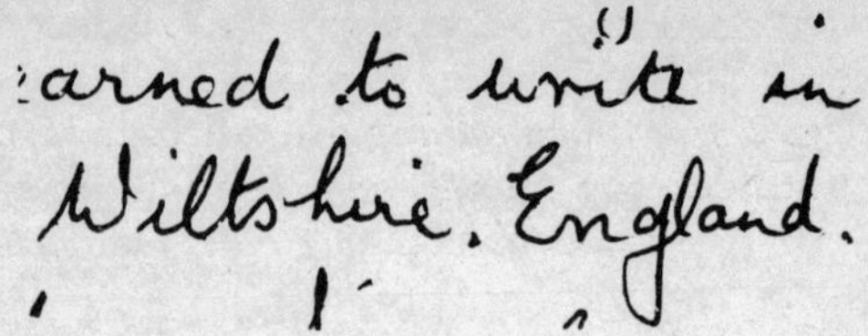

:arned to write in Wiltshire, England.

Fig. 18

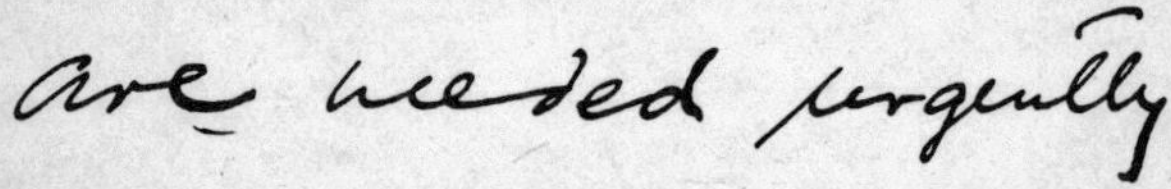

are needed urgently

Fig. 19

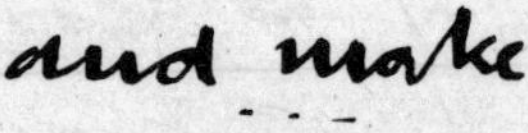

and make

Fig. 20

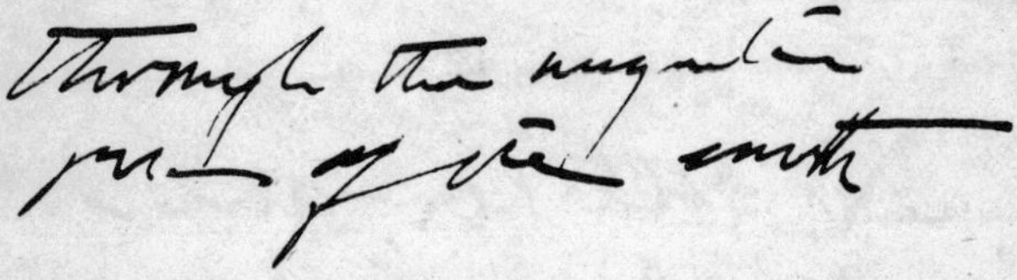

Through the negation pen of the earth

Fig. 21

10 Tension and Release

Two groups of muscles are stimulated by brain impulse to perform the act of writing, the extensor muscles which extend the fingers and the flexor muscles which draw in the fingers. Flexor muscles tense; extensor muscles release. If the brain impulse reflects emotional feelings of controlled aggression, anxiety, conflict, etc., the muscle response will be inhibited restricting the release of the extensor muscles, causing taut strokes and leftward hooks at the ends of words (Fig. 22). If the brain impulse reflects a relaxed and balanced attitude the muscle response will be balanced, flowing, rhythmic and regular (Fig. 23). Fig. 24 gives an example of extreme tension.

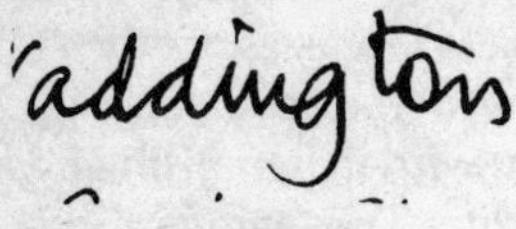

Fig. 22

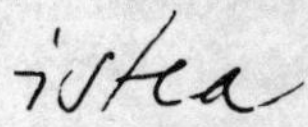

Fig. 23

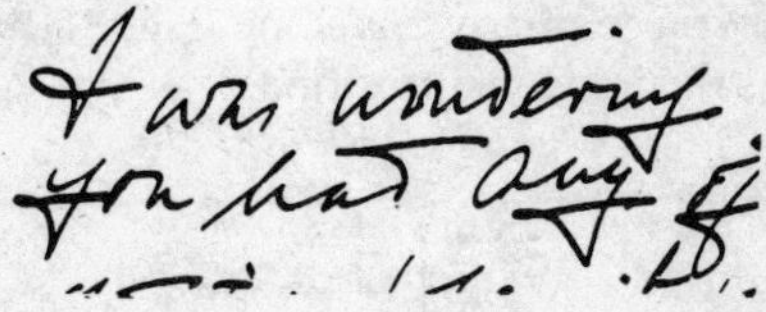

Fig. 24

11 The Envelope

Legibility on an envelope is such an obvious requirement that illegibility must point to a psychological complexity: it could be that the letter inside the envelope is of a highly emotional content and the writer's preoccupation with it overrides consideration for legibility on the envelope; it could, however, point to the writer as being an obtrusive type, tactless and possibly troublesome.

Compare the writing on an envelope (for public viewing) with that of the letter inside (for private viewing). If the writing on the envelope is small but that in the letter is larger, the writer is socially self-conscious but privately self-confident. If the writing on the envelope is larger and of greater pressure than that in the letter, the writer is determined to attract attention by calculated means.

In writing the address, a stepped design (Fig. 25) reveals an instinctive distrust of people and the need to take time to establish relationships. Fig. 26 is a block design favoured by the conventional, considerate writer. Placing the address at the top of the envelope (Fig. 27) the writer is pushing aside the realities of life and succumbing to fantasies. Conversely, in placing the address at the bottom of the envelope (Fig. 28) the writer reveals his involvement with materialism and his generally pessimistic outlook on life. The extravert pushes his address to the right (Fig. 29), the introvert to the left (Fig. 30). The exhibitionist, always eager to attract attention, makes a showpiece of any envelope (Fig. 31) and the rebel illustrates his desire to be unorthodox as in Fig. 32.

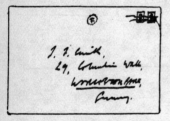

Fig. 25

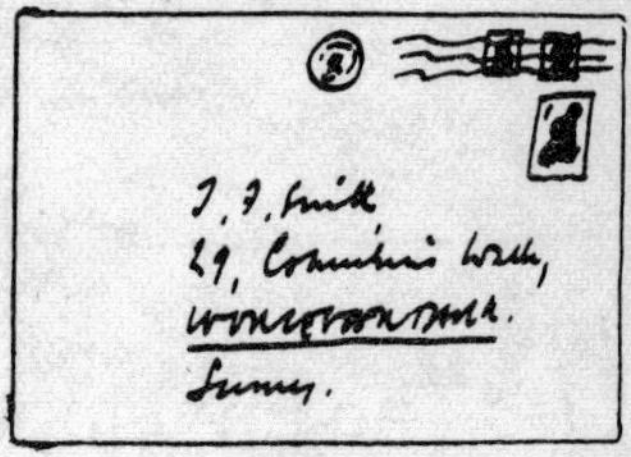

Fig. 26

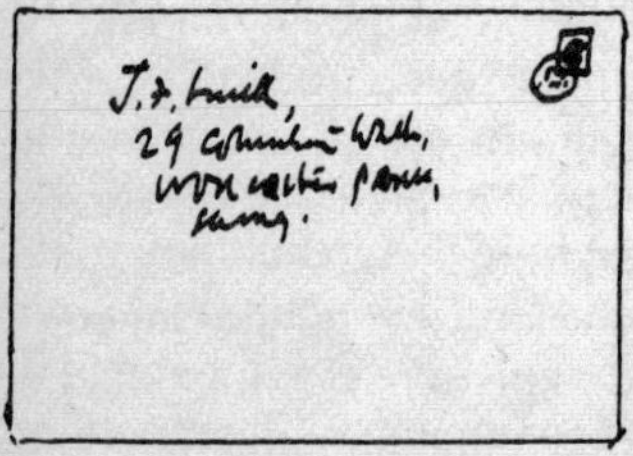

Fig. 27

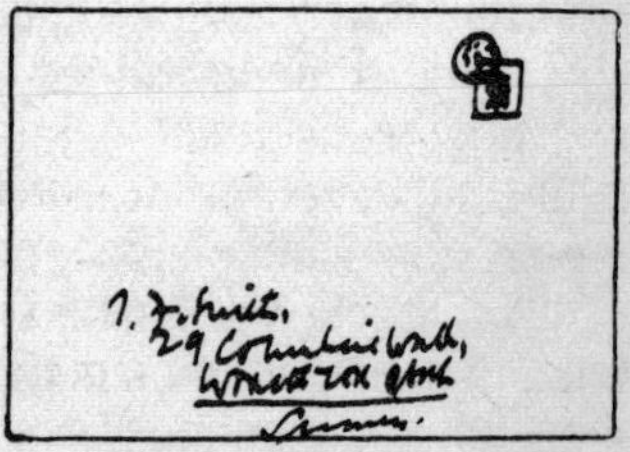

Fig. 28

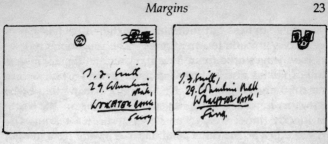

Fig. 29   Fig. 30

Fig. 31   Fig. 32

12   Margins

Margins are indicative of the writer's attitude to society.

Lack of a top margin (Fig. 33) shows a lack of respect, the writer preferring a direct and informal approach. Lack of a bottom margin (Fig. 33) reveals an inclination to lapse into dreams and sentimentality. A large top margin (Fig. 34) reflects the reserved and formal attitude of the modest, retiring type of person but a large bottom margin (Fig. 34) warns of a superficial manner. Where there are no margins at all (Fig. 35) the writer is reflecting his obsession with money and financial security: he will save every penny he can. The writer who creates wide margins on all sides (Fig. 36) seeks isolation: he is a very private person and may be inclined to morbid anxiety. A wide left margin (Fig. 37) suggests shyness but indicates that the writer has a very generous attitude towards others. The gregarious type of person leaves little room for a right margin (Fig. 38): he is full of vitality and courage but tends to act hastily. A very narrow left margin (Fig. 39) reflects a narrow mind. An irregular left margin (Fig. 40) signifies confusion: the writer is moody, indecisive, inconsistent and often fearful. The reserved, self-conscious person leaves a wide right margin (Fig. 41).

Strict control of margins always reveals self-consciousness.

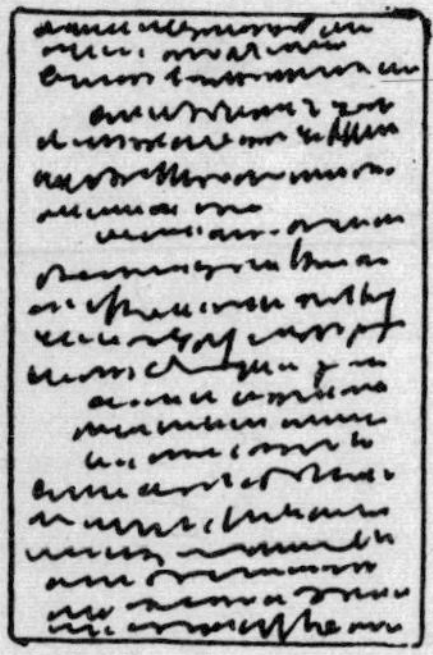

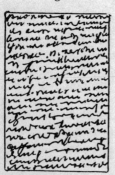

Fig. 33

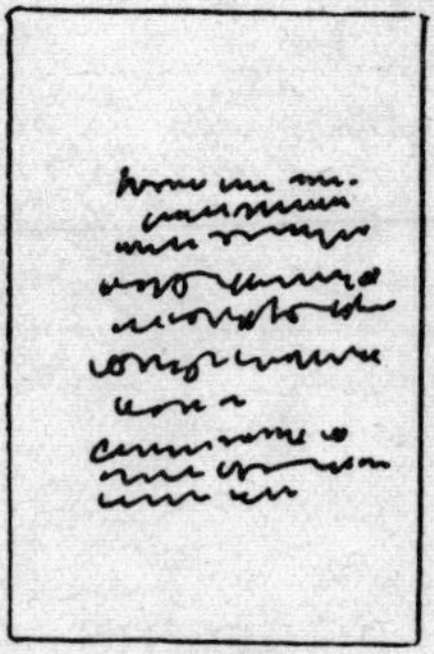

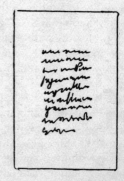

Fig. 34

Fig. 35

Fig. 36

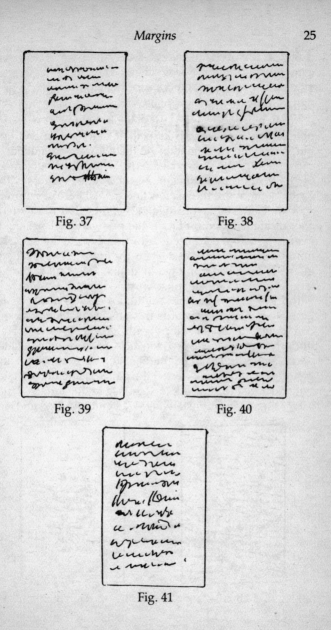

Fig. 37

Fig. 38

Fig. 39

Fig. 40

Fig. 41

13   Layout

The layout of a page of writing gives an indication of a person's ability to adapt to society.

When starting a new exercise book, note-book or diary, people usually intend to keep their writing neat and tidy but, soon, the writing takes on the natural and individual expression of the writer. Similarly, while the arrangement of the writing at the beginning of a letter expresses the writer's intention, the last few lines reveal his true nature.

A well-centred layout (Fig. 42) shows that the writer's way of life is based on order, harmony and balance: he is instinctively open-hearted towards people. The socially-minded person sets his text to the right (Fig. 43): he is interested in people and world affairs. A text set to the left (Fig. 44) reveals self-consciousness and a tendency to withdraw; the writer does not find it easy to mix socially. Lines that decrease towards the left (Fig. 45) show lack of confidence in relationships with people because of an underlying sense of suspicion held towards them. Lines decreasing towards the right (Fig. 46) indicate spontaneity, generosity and extravagance: the writer is initially reserved but warmth and confidence soon rise to the surface. Lines increasing towards the left (Fig. 47) signify shyness and lack

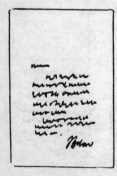

Fig. 42   Fig. 43

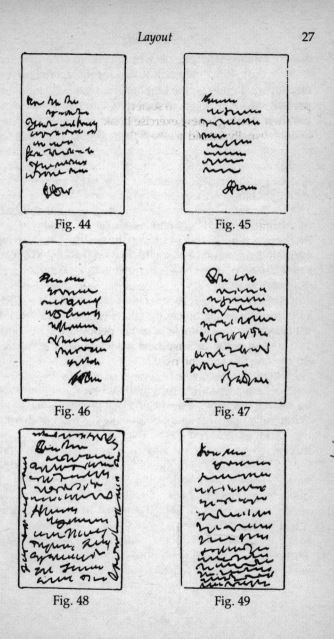

Fig. 44

Fig. 45

Fig. 46

Fig. 47

Fig. 48

Fig. 49

of spontaneity. The person who fills all the margins with writing (Fig. 48) is impractical and inconsiderate: he does not know when to stop and generally wastes time. Margin writing could indicate loneliness. Cramming lines at the foot of the page (Fig. 49) denotes sentimentality: the writer avoids making decisions and dislikes changes.

14   Spacing

Spacing between letters and words can be paralleled with pauses in speech and hesitation in gesture—it is an unconscious response to an instinctive need for selection and order. Spacing between lines, however, is a conscious and deliberate act.

Lines that are well-spaced (Fig. 50) reflect good manners, self-assurance and reveal excellent business abilities. An unusually deep spacing between lines is a sign of inferiority and indicates that person who pretends to be what he is not.

Frequently large spaces between letters inside words (Fig. 51) reflect sudden stops in the thought process caused by mental overstrain—a warning of a possible breakdown. When only one such space occurs in a piece of handwriting the thought flow obviously has been interrupted by a momentary external cause. Irregular spaces between words (Fig. 52) indicate an emotionally unstable personality: the writer's feelings are poorly controlled, his judgement vague, his demeanour excitable and confused. Very large, regular spaces between words (Fig. 53) suggest an aversion to social relationships and a desire for isolation. Conversely, where there are no spaces between words (Fig. 54) the writer is expressing his desire to be close to people and his need to identify himself with a group—the herd instinct.

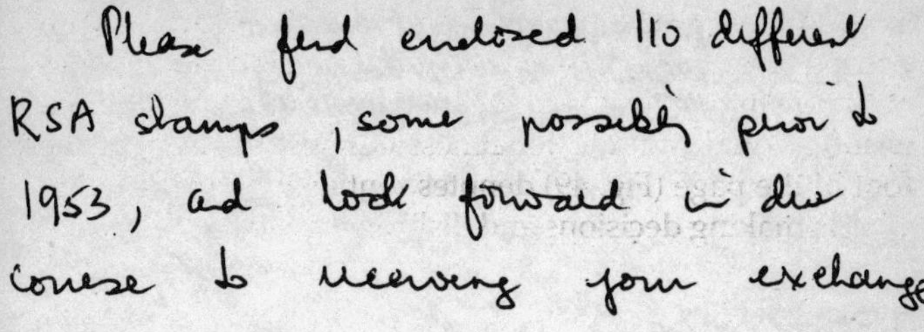

Please fend enclosed 110 different
RSA stamps, some possibly prior to
1953, and look forward in due
course to receiving your exchange

Fig. 50

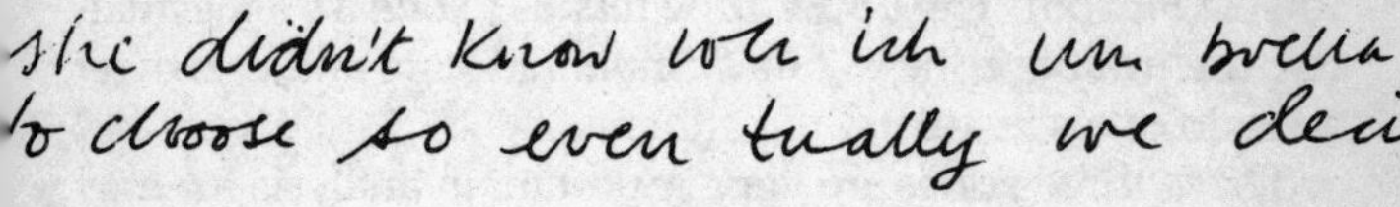

she didn't know wch ish um brella
to choose so even tually we deci

Fig. 51

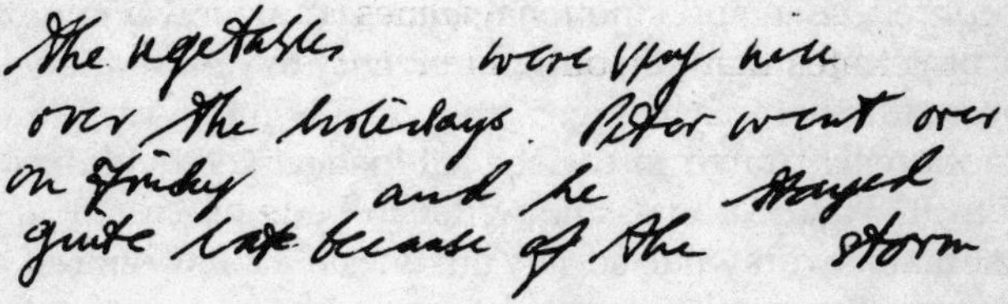

The vegetables   were vfry nice
over the holidays. Pdor went over
on friday   and he   stayed
quite late because of the   storm

Fig. 52

he   came   back   or
went   over   to
first   gear.   Ever

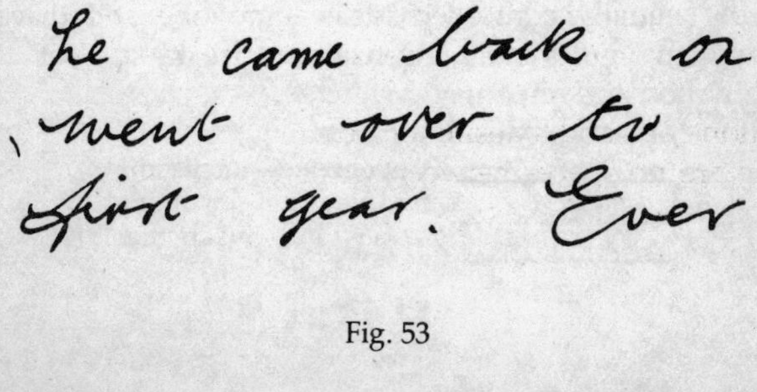

Fig. 53

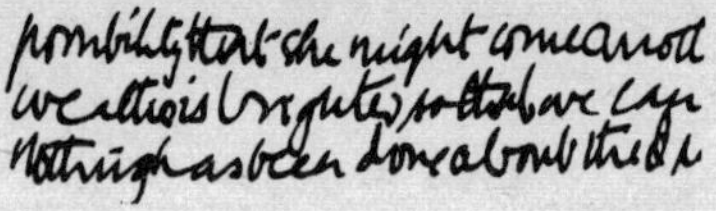

Fig. 54

15   Zones

There are three zones in handwriting: upper, middle and
lower (Fig. 55). The upper zone relates to one's intellectuality, the middle zone to one's emotional state and the lower
zone to one's instincts.

These three zones are very important in analysis for they
may vary in direction and length and thus reveal com-
plexities of the mind. For example, in Fig. 56 the upper and
middle zones are leaning to the left, signifying inhibitions in
the intellectual and emotional areas but the lower zone is
turning to the right revealing a tendency towards society in
the instinctual area. In Fig. 57 the writer is intellectually and
emotionally drawn to society but instinctively withdraws
from it. Fig. 58 shows the writer to be intellectually and
instinctively drawn to society but does not allow himself to
become emotionally involved.

Script or uniform writing (Fig. 59) reflects an equable
temperament. The writer takes a pride in careful symmetry
and methodical hard work but the equally controlled zones,
i.e. the equally controlled ideas, emotions and drives,
reveal an inflexible, insensitive streak—a lack of
imagination and impetus.

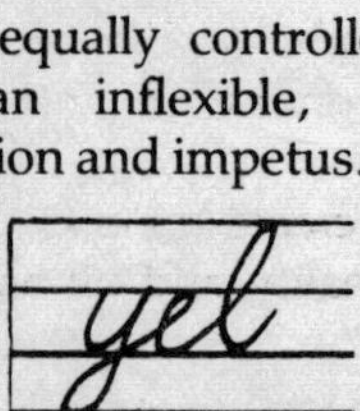

upper zone—intellectual
middle zone—emotional
lower zone—instinctual

Fig. 55

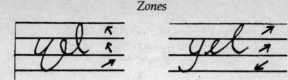

| Fig. 56 | Fig. 57 |

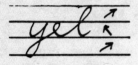

| Fig. 58 | Fig. 59 |

UPPER ZONE

The upper zone (the area of imagination, intellect, fantasies and religious inclinations), must be carefully considered in analysis: it must always be compared with the other two zones for signs of dominance or weakness. In Fig. 60, for example, the high upper projections and large middle zone dominate the lower zone, which is small (weak). Prominence is given to an emotionally-coloured imagination lacking the balance of a long lower zone which would have produced a moderating effect.

Very high projections accompanied by a small middle zone and a very short lower zone would produce an emphasized dominance in the upper zone and dramatic loss of balance with the other two zones. A vivid imagination would allow the writer to create his own world by easily substituting fantasy for reality and all aspirations would be thwarted by lack of self-confidence and drive.

A lack of upper zone projections (Fig. 61) reveals a lack of upper zone qualities: a dull person whose interests are purely materialistic.

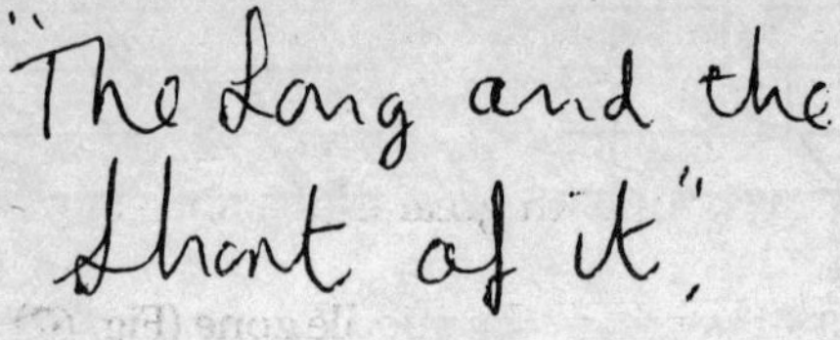

"The Long and the Short of it".

Fig. 60

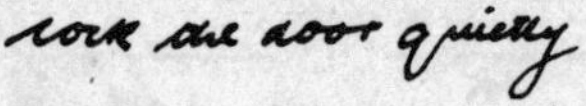

lock the door quietly

Fig. 61

MIDDLE ZONE

The middle zone is the area of emotional attitudes—
perception, self-awareness, adaptation to reality, memory,
etc.—and, because the ego is involved, it is important to
note not only the direction of the letters (left, suppressed
ego; right, expressed ego) but also their size (large, inflated
ego; small, deflated ego). The letters i and m are the best
consistent representatives of the general size of middle
zone letters in a piece of handwriting. Measurements are
made in millimetres.

Letters of approximately ½mm. reveal an unemotional,
highly objective personality; such extremely small writing
suggests acute observation of detail. Depression can reduce
the size of writing and any sample of writing consisting of
letters less than 3mm. should be compared with samples
from different periods to see if the smallness is consistent or
temporary. A small middle zone indicates self-control,
concentration and a modest disposition.

A good ego balance occurs at approximately 3mm.
revealing adaptability, self-confidence and a positive
attitude to the realities of life; 4mm. and over denotes an
inflated ego: everything the writer says or does is
exaggerated and his extreme subjectivity and excessive self-

assertiveness make it difficult for others to tolerate him. At 8mm. and over the writer is revealing an overrated self-importance: the emotions are highly exaggerated and all activity is carried out with great exuberance but with little thought behind it.

Uniformity of height in the middle zone (Fig. 62) denotes total self-confidence and emotional control—a firm, just character. A strongly-emphasized middle zone, diminishing both the upper and lower zones (Fig. 63) signifies complacency: the writer is only interested in 'now' and goes through life taking everything for granted.

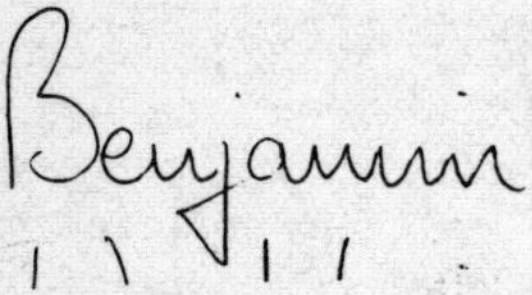

Fig. 62

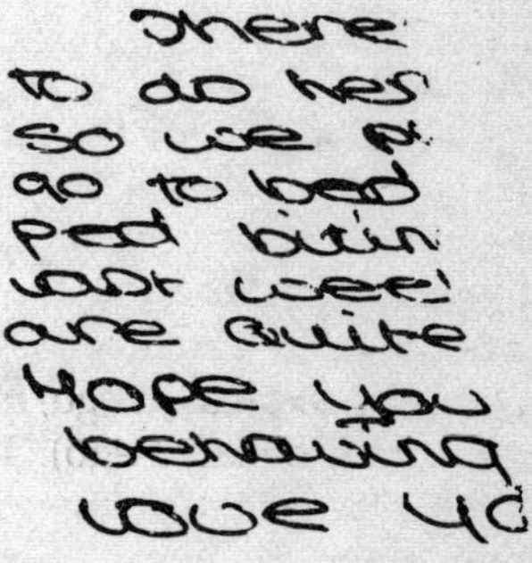

Fig. 63

LOWER ZONE

The lower zone (the area of the unconscious) represents drives (need-activity-gratification) and instincts (excitation of feeling directed to an objective).

A dominant lower zone (Fig. 64) reveals a physically vigorous person who has good athletic ability and a strong sexual drive. A stunted lower zone indicates lack of interest in material needs: sexual drive is repressed. Heavy pressure in a long, lower zone (Fig. 65) signifies material interests; light pressure, a constant desire for financial security.

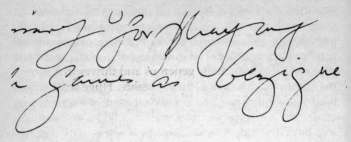

Fig. 64

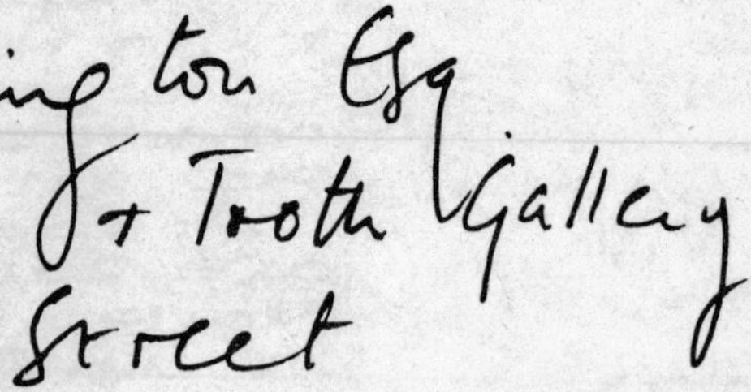

Fig. 65

16 Size

The size of writing, i.e. the visual effect of all three zones together forming a whole, gives a general indication of the writer's personality.

Extremely small writing (Fig. 66) always indicates a high intelligence and the ability to concentrate totally on a matter to the exclusion of everything else. Small writing reveals shrewdness, acute perception and morality: an inhibiting modesty suppresses emotion, dispels ambition and undermines self-confidence. Large, rapid writing with evenly-controlled proportions shows great will power: an outgoing, enterprising person with natural personal superiority. Large writing which is spontaneous and unrestrained signifies the exhibitionist: always striving to impress, he is vivacious, generous and thrives in a state of megalomania preferring to shun reality. Huge writing (Fig. 67) reveals a totally subjective attitude to all things.

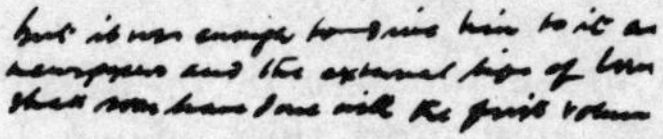

Fig. 66

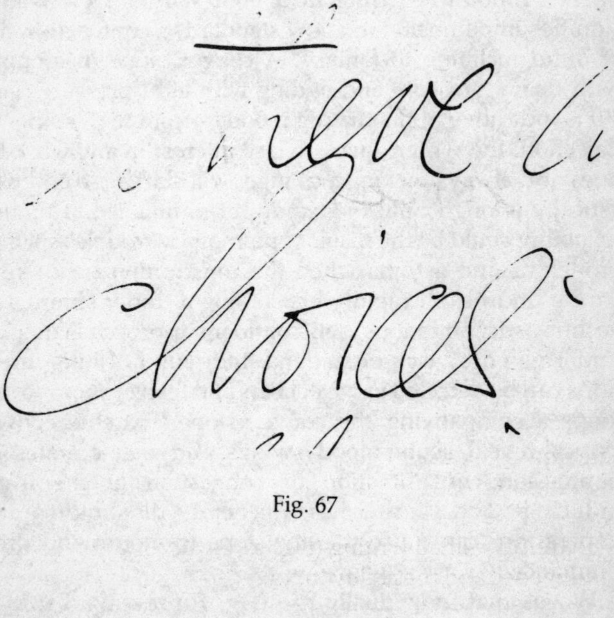

Fig. 67

17 Slopes

Slopes are indicative of a person's mental or physical condition.

UPWARD SLOPES

Rising slopes are expressive of optimism, enthusiasm, energy and determination (Fig. 68) and, if constantly maintained in a high standard of handwriting, reveal a great capacity for hard work and an eagerness for enterprise. Pronounced rising in a high standard of writing signifies impetuosity; in a low standard, a confused frame of mind inclining to fantasy. A convex slope, beginning with heavy pressure and ending with light pressure (Fig. 69) is indicative of fluctuating moods—from high spirits to dejection: the writer, quick to lose interest in any work he does and always seeking a change, will start a job enthusiastically enough only to abandon it unfinished. This unreliability could be the result of pulmonary troubles such as bronchitis and asthma when the constitution is not very strong and health rapidly breaks down under strain; any enthusiastic, ambitious, self-confident approach is quickly undermined by lack of stamina. Indication of lung infections can be detected in weak t bars and feeble, short, lower loops accompanying the convex slope. Extreme convex slopes reveal acute mood swings and manic states of depression. Inflammation or congestion of the liver, inducing bad headaches, general discomfort and depression, can cause the line slope to mount and drop dramatically.

Words that individually rise (Fig. 70) reveal a battle to overcome ill-health. The writer lacks the stamina to keep the word on a level base but resolutely pulls the beginning of each word back to line.

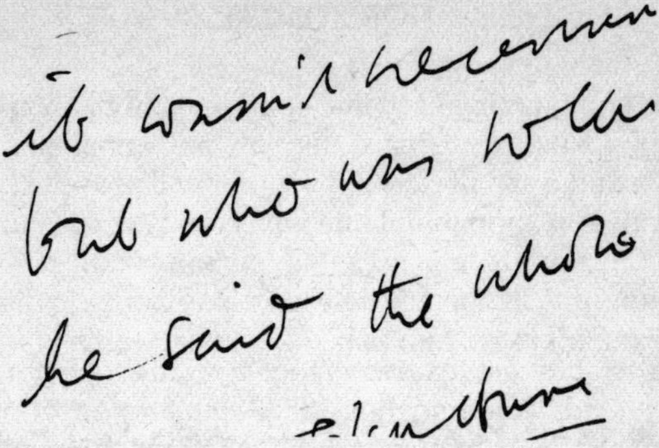

it wasn't because
but who was told
he said the whole
e.l.m.throw

Fig. 68

associated with good it is things
he may have been a means
to Southern area. The work was
being done in the middle ages
after the monks of Kiri robba
it is that like panel.

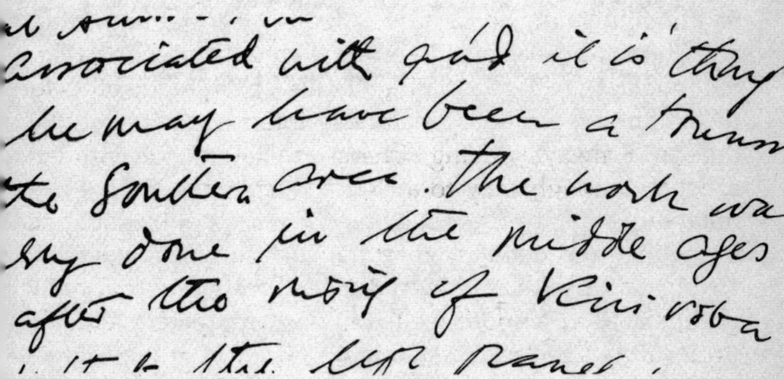

Fig. 69

I hope all is well

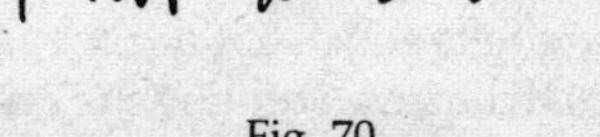

Fig. 70

HORIZONTAL

Consistently writing each line on an even horizontal course (Fig. 71) shows persistence, tenacity and constancy. If the letters a and o are all closed the writer will prove to be loyal and honest. A horizontal line which wavers up and down (Fig. 72) reveals an excitable person with poor self-discipline; quick mood changes and a readiness to disregard arrangements mark him as being unreliable.

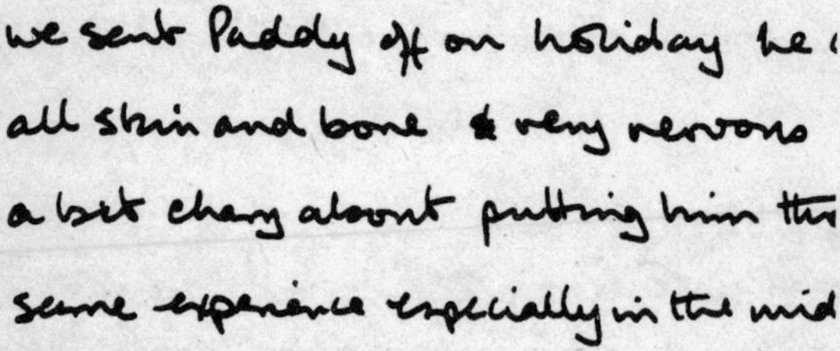

we sent Paddy off on holiday he
all skin and bone & very nervous
a bit chary about putting him th
same experience especially in the mid

Fig. 71

Hope to see you some

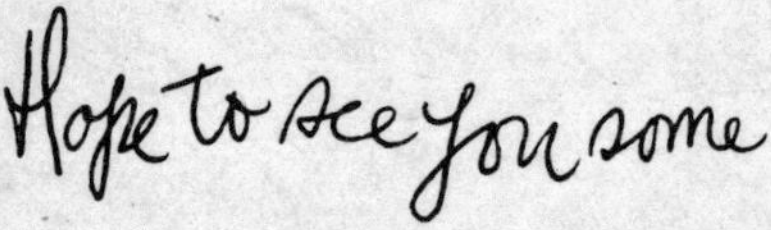

Fig. 72

WRITING ON LINED PAPER

If the handwriting falls consistently above the printed line (Fig. 73) the writer has an enthusiastic nature; below the printed line (Fig. 74) reveals a matter-of-fact, materialistic person. Meandering over the printed line (Fig. 75) suggests an upset state of mind and a strong feeling of insecurity.

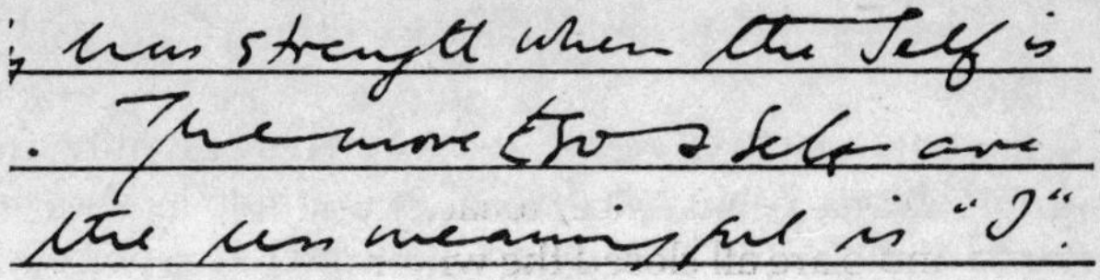

[handwritten text, Fig. 73]

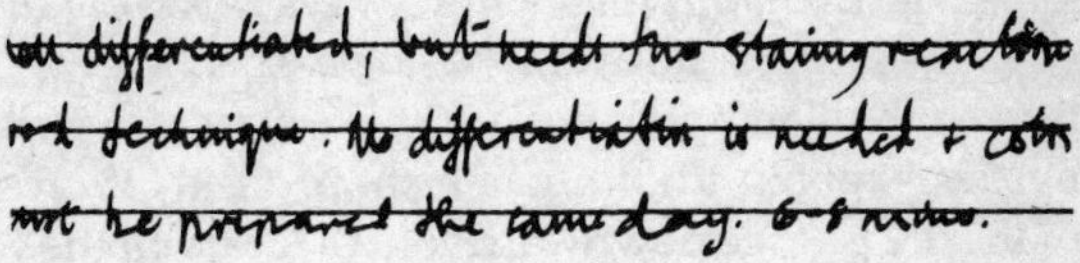

Fig. 73

[handwritten text with strikethrough, Fig. 74]

Fig. 74

[handwritten text, Fig. 75]

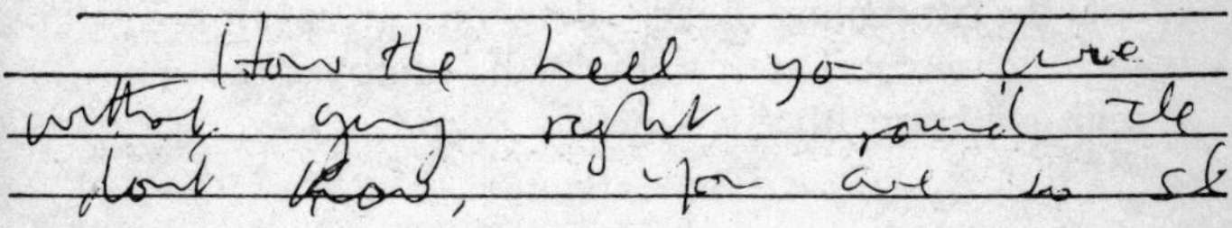

Fig. 75

DOWNWARD SLOPE

Lines or words that slope downwards indicate, in varying degrees, tiredness, depression, deliberate concealment or lack of foresight. It is wise to have examples of writing from different times to observe consistencies or differentiations: deliberate concealment, for example, is not likely to be a consistent trait; depression, however, could be consistent.

Words that droop at the end of a line (Fig. 76) indicate tiredness: if the slope continues to droop downwards dramatically the writer must be exhausted but if the drooping occurs during the first lines of writing only, the writer is more likely to be feeling dejected than tired. Drooping at the end of a line in order to squash in the end of a word (Fig. 77) reveals the time-wasting person who always leaves things until the last minute, i.e. lack of foresight.

It is preferable to compare several pieces of writing from different times when faced with an example as shown in Fig. 78 for this could be a 'mood' slope merely representing a current feeling of depression or sadness. If it is consistent in different writings it reveals a very depressed state of mind. A concave slope (Fig. 79) is always representative of a victory over pessimism or weakness: however much caution or vacillation takes place at the start, the writer can always be relied upon to finish a task. Words that dramatically plunge downwards out of line with the writing reveal a very deep depression and indicate suicidal tendencies (Fig. 80). Descending letters in words (Fig. 81) reveal the concealing of facts: the writer gives himself away by a psychological 'jerk' in much the same way as one who is telling an untruth involuntarily gulps.

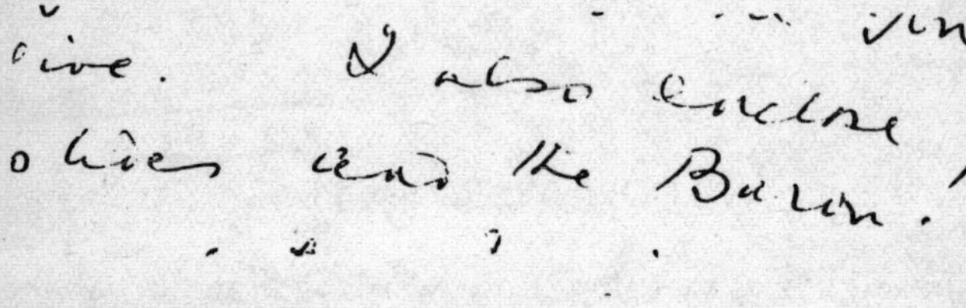

Fig. 76

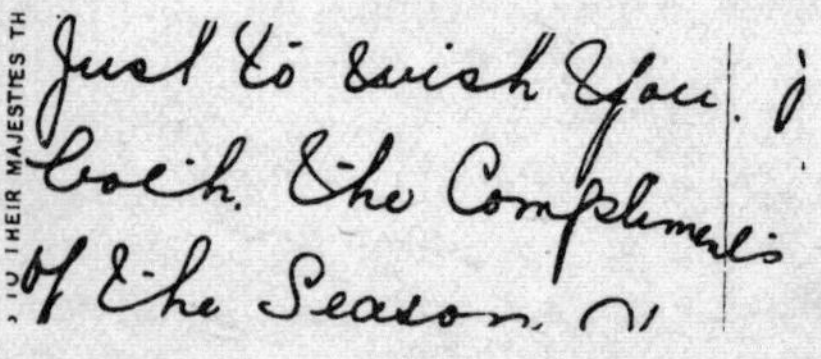

Fig. 77

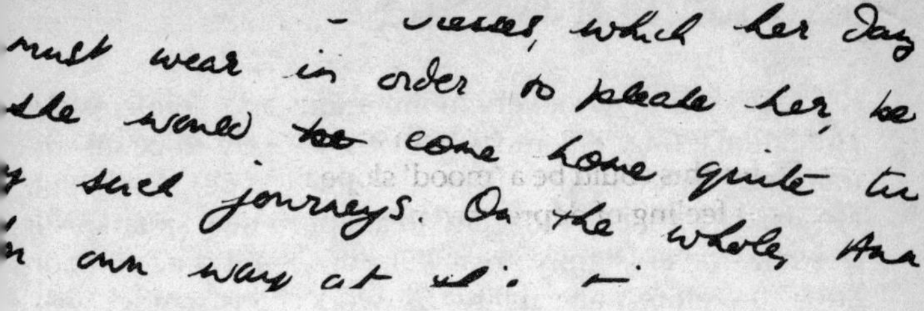

— ..esses, which her day
must wear in order to please her, be
she would ... come home quite ti..
.. such journeys. On the whole, Ana
.. own way at wi.. ..

Fig. 78

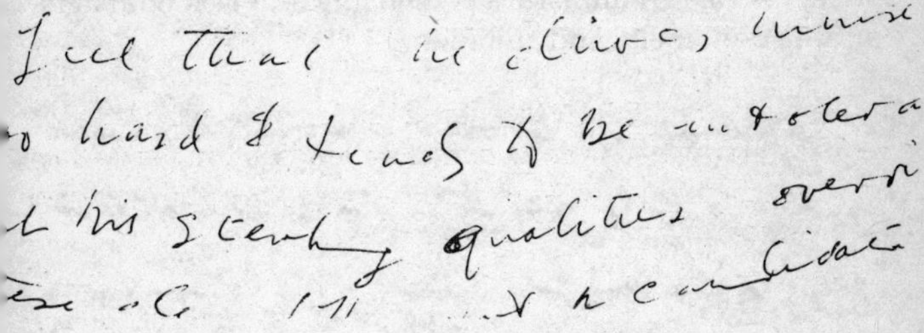

I ... that he lives, minus
.. hard & tends to be intolera
.. his sterling qualities overri
.. .. a candidate

Fig. 79

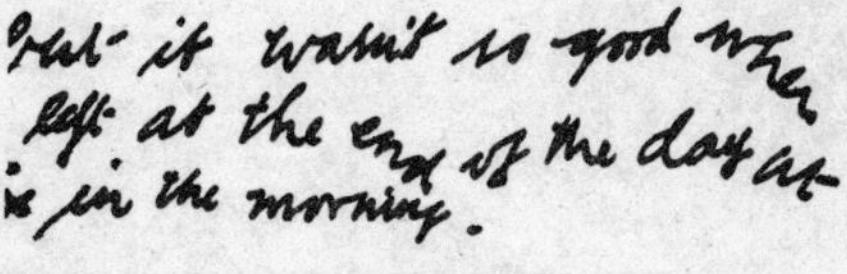

..but it wasn't so good when
.. at the end of the day ..
.. in the morning.

Fig. 80

well here I am
..ery jolly time ..

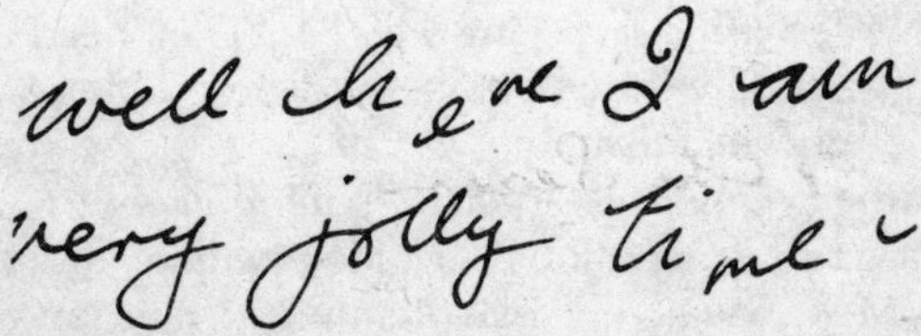

Fig. 81

18 Regular Writing

Regular writing has a very monotonous and uninteresting appearance (Fig. 82) and the writer is likely to be an unimaginative, melancholic, plodding type. Although regularity reveals an inability to adapt to new situations it does, however, signify great will-power and concentration and, therefore, an ability to work consistently well. Handwriting develops and changes with maturity so that regular writing, done by an adult who retains a copybook style, reveals an immature personality and lack of imagination, spontaneity and ambition.

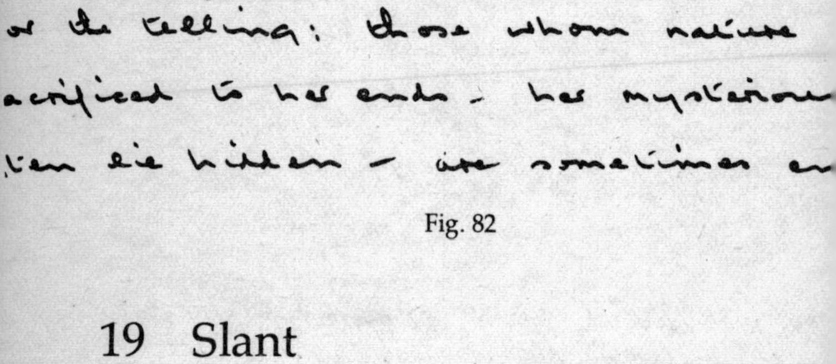

or the telling: those whom nature sacrificed to her ends – her mysterious ten die hidden – are sometimes en

Fig. 82

19 Slant

LEFT: THE INTROVERT

Socially reticent, self-absorbed, undemonstrative, sensitive people write with a left slant (Fig. 83). They need understanding friends who will have to tolerate little consideration and much egotism.

In young people the left slant is more likely to indicate repressions or frustrations; in older people, disappointments. Men usually display feminine traits and fussy attitudes; women, masculine traits and cold, deliberate attitudes.

The degree of slant suggests the degree of withdrawal from society (Fig. 84). A slant of 130° is shown in Fig. 85. An extreme leftward slant, i.e. below 140° is found in the handwriting of those who automatically oppose everything and everyone: it is a pointer to unhappiness in the formative years—the writer is withdrawn, unadaptable, detached and intensely emotional.

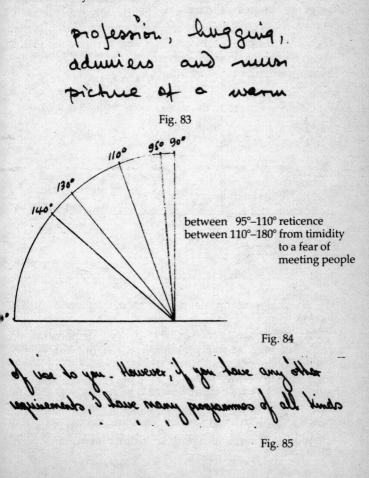

Fig. 83

between 95°–110° reticence
between 110°–180° from timidity
to a fear of
meeting people

Fig. 84

Fig. 85

PERPENDICULAR

The degrees of slant in perpendicular or upright writing is shown in Fig. 86. The perpendicular slant (Fig. 87), always restrains emotions and those who use the upright will have a certain coldness and aloofness in their character: they have charm, poise and good manners but their friendship never encourages intimacy.

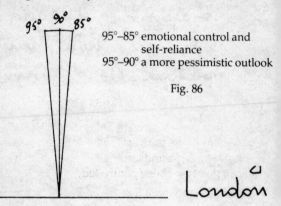

95°–85° emotional control and
self-reliance
95°–90° a more pessimistic outlook

Fig. 86

Fig. 87

RIGHT: THE EXTRAVERT

Fig. 88 illustrates the degrees of slant mentioned in this section.

The right slant reveals the active, demonstrative, impulsive type. Heavy pressure in the right slant always intensifies emotions and signifies absolute sincerity and a strong sense of justice. The more extravert the person, the larger will be the writing. The intellectual extravert will write in a smallish, concentrated hand.

An average right slant of 85°–80° (Fig. 89) reveals the friendly, sympathetic nature of a broad-minded, honest person who takes life in his stride. At 70°–65° (Fig. 90) and slightly more extravert, the writer is gregarious, very affectionate and full of optimism, enthusiasm and energy. A right slant of 65°–50° (Fig. 91) reveals a very excitable and highly enthusiastic nature: the need for the company of other people is paramount. A slant of 50° (Fig. 92) signifies a totally reckless and credulous nature and is indicative of drinking problems. All slants from 50°–0°, which are extreme, reflect unrestrained behaviour and delusions of grandeur.

Variation of slant (Fig. 93) is indicative of an indecisive mood caused by a fluctuation in emotions. A word starting with a perpendicular stroke and developing a rightward slant (Fig. 94) shows self-control giving way to excitement (a good example of this is illustrated in Fig. 95 where the writer, obviously affected by mentioning South Africa, suddenly swings from a consistently 95°–90° slant to a 70° slant). A word starting with a rightward slant and developing a perpendicular slant (Fig. 96) shows that an initial impulse has been controlled.

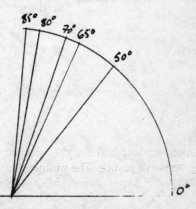

Fig. 88

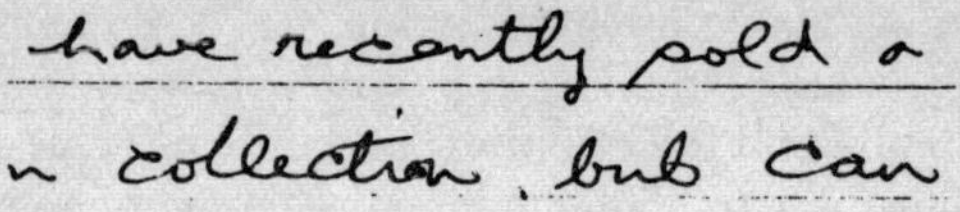

have recently sold a
n collection, but can

Fig. 89

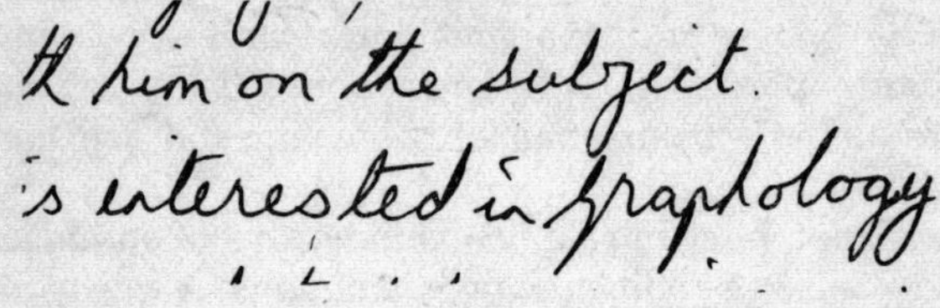

th him on the subject.
is interested in graphology

Fig. 90

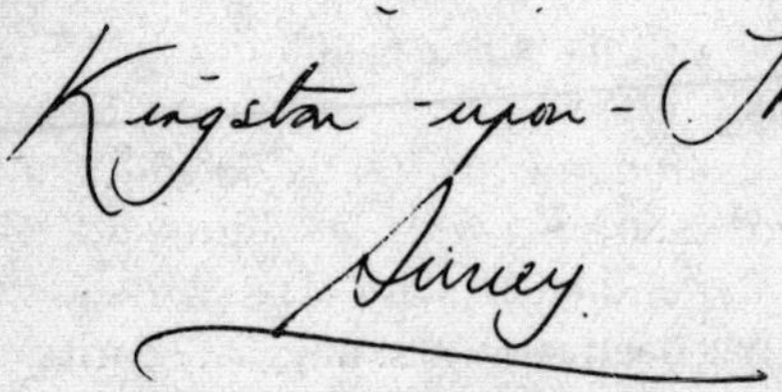

Kingston -upon- Thames,
Surrey

Fig. 91

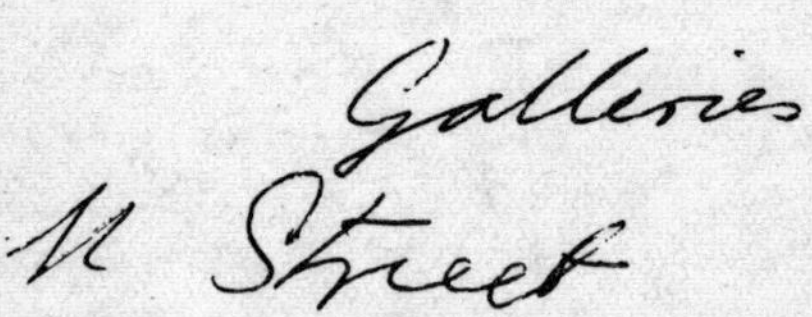

Galleries
11 Street

Fig. 92

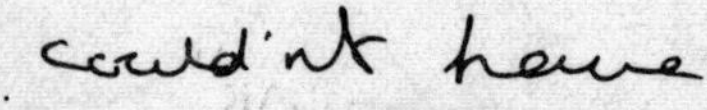

could'nt have

Fig. 93

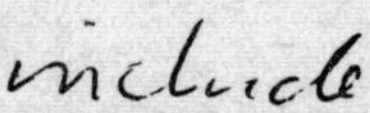

include

Fig. 94

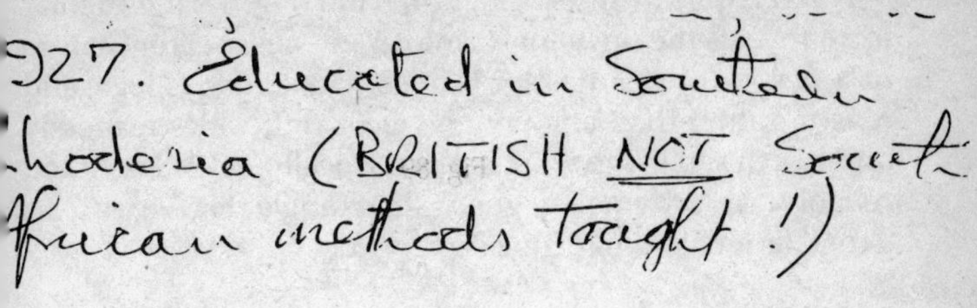

927. Educated in Southern
Rhodesia (BRITISH NOT South
African methods taught !)

Fig. 95

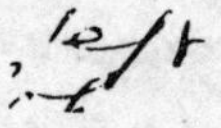

Fig. 96

20 Connective Forms

There are four connective forms: angular, garland, arcade
and thread. They are indicative of a person's disposition
and social adaptability. The majority of handwritings have a
predominant connective form; the introduction and
frequency of other connective forms and their effect on
fluency must be studied carefully—a consistent variation
which does not interrupt the flow or legibility of the writing
reveals great diversification of character. Connective forms
which disturb the natural flow must be negatively interpreted (see 'Counter-strokes'—section 35).

ANGULAR

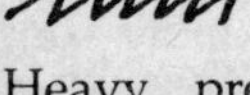

A positive movement characteristic of a strong
decisive mind and disciplined character.
Heavy pressure in angular handwriting signifies a
domineering attitude.

Written quickly in a small, firm hand (Fig. 97) the angular form reveals the unyielding, intolerant, almost cruel nature of a person of steadfast principles who employs logic and reason rather than emotion: he faces difficulties fearlessly and has the ability to work enthusiastically, relentlessly and reliably. An extremely regular, sharp angle (Fig. 98) reveals a total lack of spontaneous expression.

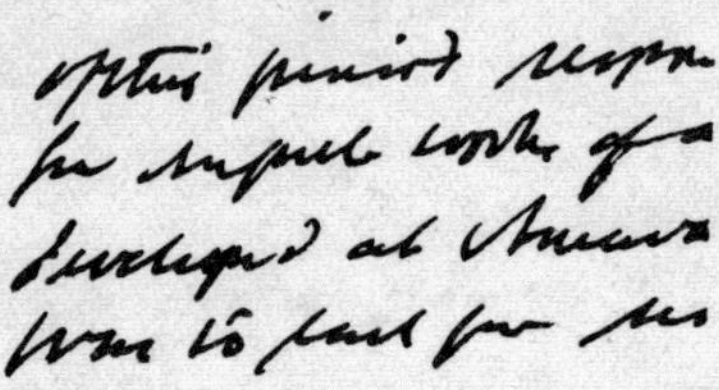

Fig. 97

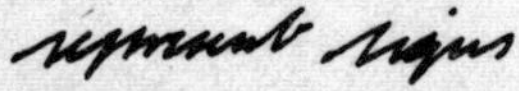

Fig. 98

GARLAND

a submissive movement used by those of a trusting, sympathetic and gentle disposition.

A rhythmic flow, as in Fig. 99, reflects the vigour of a selfless, proficient person; the rhythm maintained in joining words (Fig. 100) emphasizes altruism without sentimentality. The flat-based garland (Fig. 101) is used by freedom-loving, unprejudiced, progressive people. The deeply curved garland (Fig. 102) indicates a more contemplative and serious type. Superfluous garlands (Fig. 103) suggests an ingratiating manner.

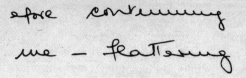

Fig. 99

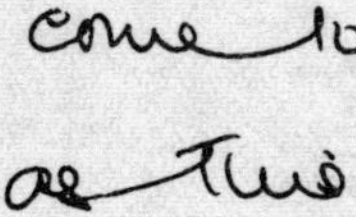

come to

as this

Fig. 100

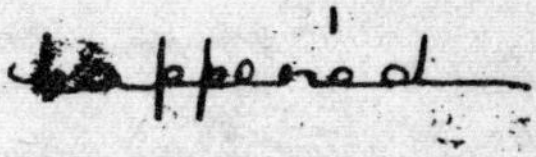

Fig. 101

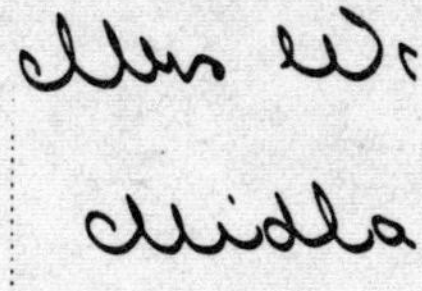

Fig. 102

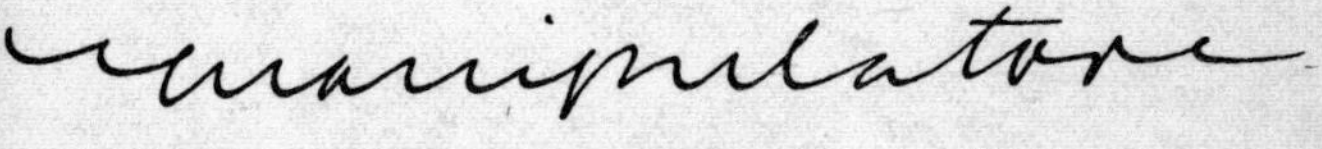

Fig. 103

ARCADE

The arcade connective form (Fig. 104) is a secretive movement; the arc is like a lid covering emotions, hiding reactions and concealing calculations. It is characteristic of those who tend towards insincerity and, if written slowly with a left slant, it suggests mendacity and hypocrisy.

Fig. 105 shows an initial arcade letter followed by a different connective form (garland). The arcade, being a slower movement than the other forms of connection, makes this initial letter the bow or handshake before conversation—an expression of respect. In Fig. 106 the final letter in a garland connective form becomes an arcade causing a sudden braking effect and suppressing what normally would have been a spontaneous, outgoing stroke. This defensive impulse reveals confusion or insincerity.

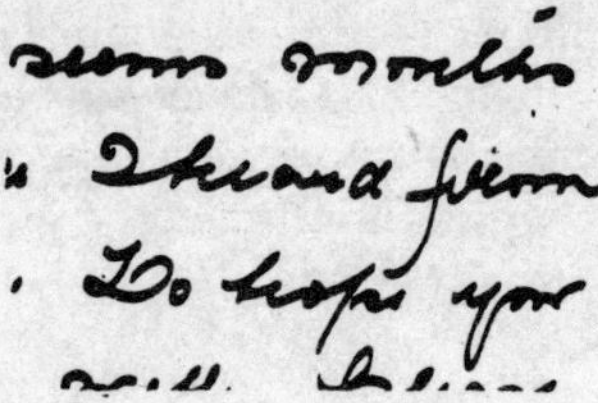

Fig. 104

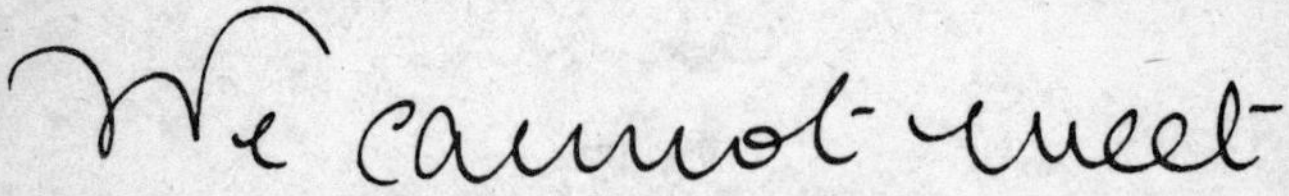

Fig. 105

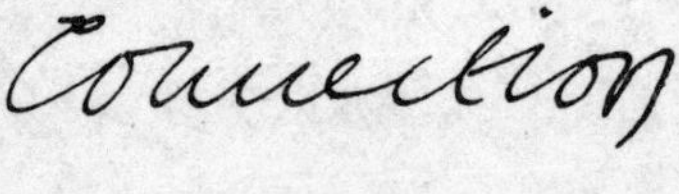

Fig. 106

THREAD

A formless, straggling movement which generally indicates obscurity: the writer has no intention of divulging his thoughts to anyone.

Threads within words (Fig. 107) occur in speed writing when thoughts often run ahead of the pen, the thread being a 'catching-up' process; they also reflect the writer's volubility and penchant for dramatic descriptions but, however talkative, the writer gives very little, if anything, away. If the threads have no pressure, as in Fig. 107, the writer is an opportunist; heavy pressure reveals an instinctive desire for freedom—the writer hates to be bound by rules. Words ending in threads (Fig. 108) show powerful intuition, clever repartee and the ability to evade predicaments: a generally nonchalant attitude is reflected in the writer's appearance. If the thread ending points towards the lower zone, as in Fig. 108, it denotes rebellious instincts; if it points towards the upper zone, the ability to satisfactorily tie up loose ends is indicated.

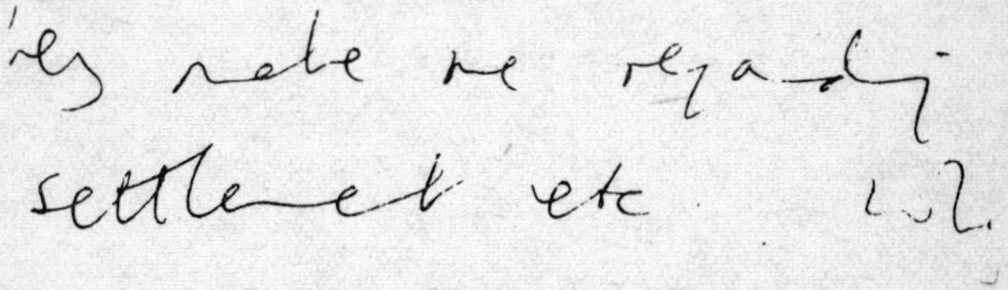

Fig. 107

Fig. 108

21 Linear Patterns

EMBELLISHMENTS

People who are attracted to vulgarity and pretentious qualities adorn their handwriting with scrolls, flourishes and elaborate curves (Fig. 109).

SIMPLIFICATION

The breaking-down of letters to a basic simple form (Fig. 110) reflects the critical, austere nature and exceptional self-discipline of the writer.

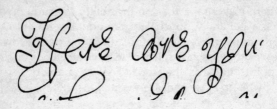

Fig. 109

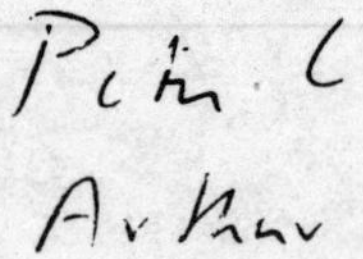

Fig. 110

22 Pictorial Patterns

FIGURES

Letters that resemble figures (Fig. 111) indicate that the writer has an interest in, or frequent viewing of, figures. Fig. 112 shows the capital L in the signature of a young man whose ambition it is to be very wealthy: he has unconsciously turned his L into a pound sign. The lower case f in Fig. 113 written by a picture dealer also resembles a pound sign.

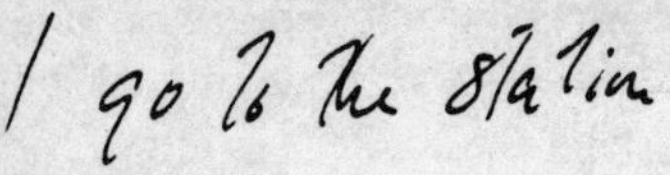

I go to the station

Fig. 111    Fig. 112    Fig. 113

MUSICAL NOTES AND SYMBOLS

The letters in Fig. 114 resemble musical notes and are indicative of interest in, or connection with, music. The musical symbol for the sharp # can be seen incorporated in the signatures of Gluck, Haydn, Felicien David and Beethoven (Figs. 115 a.b.c.d.).

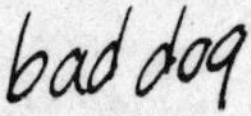

bad dog

Fig. 114 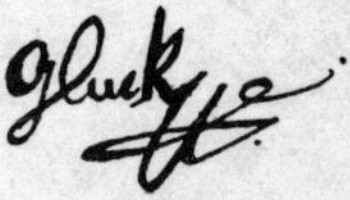   Fig. 115a

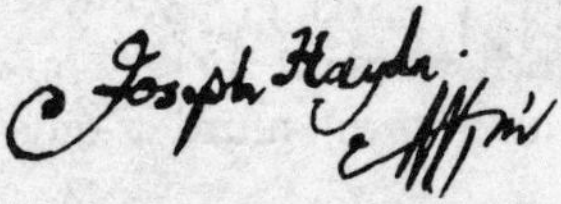

Fig. 115b

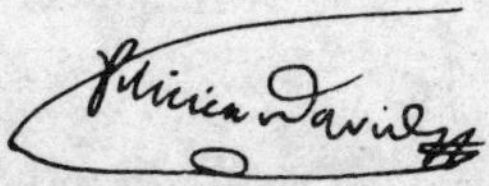

Fig. 115c

Fig. 115d

SEXUAL SYMBOLS

Frequent appearances of the symbols in Fig. 116 (or if they are prominently displayed) indicate a proclivity for sexual excesses.

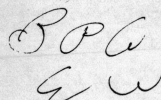

Fig. 116

WEAPONS

The letter forms, F, t, J, (dagger, whip, sword) in Fig. 117 appear in the handwriting of those who have a violent or cruel nature. Thoughts of murder or suicide are easily aroused.

Fig. 117

As well as musicians, people in expressive or physical jobs

often unconsciously incorporate their signatures a flourish descriptive of movements displayed in their work or of instruments they use. As an example Figs. 118 and 119 show the initial letters of the signatures of Floyd Patterson and Emile Griffith: they reflect characteristic movements made by the men in the ring. Figs. 120 a.b.c.d. show the initial letters taken from the signatures of boxers: they all symbolize the boxing glove. Fig. 121 shows the endstroke of an artist's signature, symbolizing the palette.

Fig. 118

Fig. 119

Fig. 120a 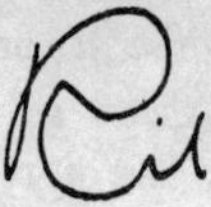   Fig. 120b    Fig. 120c

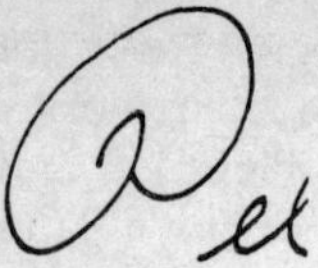

Fig. 120d 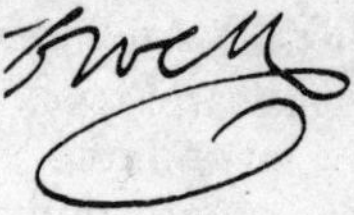   Fig. 121

23   Ink Colour

Choice of ink colour is an unconscious but positive statement by the writer of his attitude in society.

Red   reflects the impulse to shock in order to draw attention to the writer who has an intense desire to experience everything.

Violet   is favoured by the emotionally immature and the fashion-conscious: in men it reveals foppishness or effeminacy; in women, gracefulness and a love for high society.

Green   expresses the desire to impress—superior, autocratic, reformative, moralizing.

Brown   reveals sensationalism and a need for security and contentment.

Light blue   is favoured by the gentle, intellectual type

Dark blue   reflects a calm, trusting nature and a conventional outlook.

Black   is chosen by the demanding, possessive type; always decisive.

Intense black   signifies a sensual, rebellious, depressive nature.

The use of two or more different colours in one piece of writing indicates a mental disorder.

24   Connection and Disconnection

Connection signifies logic; disconnection, intuition.

In the upper zone (intellectuality) connected letters denote a continuous thought process (Fig. 122); disconnected letters denote intuition (Fig. 123). In the middle zone (emotion) connected letters reveal social adaptability (Fig. 124); disconnected letters suggest a lack of ability to adapt (Fig. 125). In the lower zone (instinct) connected letters indicate a natural friendliness (Fig. 126); disconnected letters indicate reserve (Fig. 127).

Letters within words that are constantly linked (Fig. 128) indicate the careful, practical person: lacking initiative and intuition he deals with matters in a systematical, logical way. Letters in words that are constantly separated (Fig. 129) reveal a creative individual full of imagination and ideas but liable to jump to conclusions and to make hasty decisions on the strength of instinct and intuition: he is not a sociable person and tends to avoid relationships, preferring isolation. Occurring in lines that rise this type of writing indicates a clear vision and great optimism.

A flow of writing extending from one word to another (Fig. 130) reveals the quick thought of a very active mind. Fig. 131, in contrast, shows the slow, groping efforts of an indecisive mind: each full stop represents a long pause while the writer thinks of what to put next. A definite gap between the first letter and the remainder of a word (Fig. 132) signifies caution and procrastination. The gap appearing between the word and its last letter (Fig. 133) is caused by hesitation: the writer checks and re-checks everything; he will consider and re-consider before deciding anything.

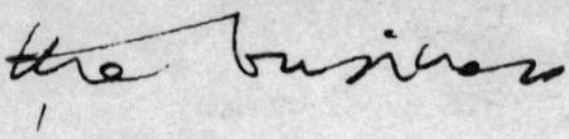

the business

Fig. 122

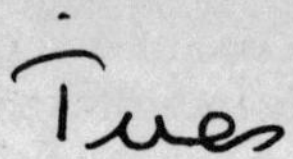

Tues

Fig. 123

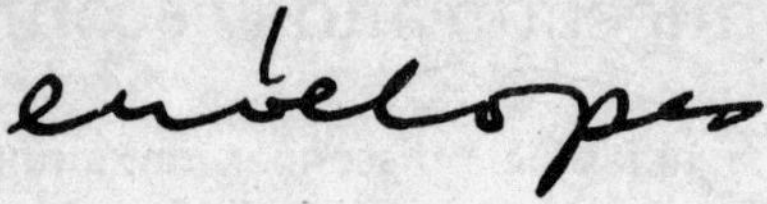

envelopes

Fig. 124

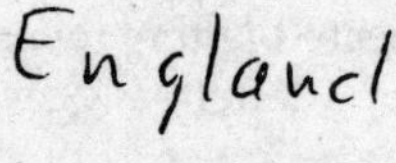

England

Fig. 125

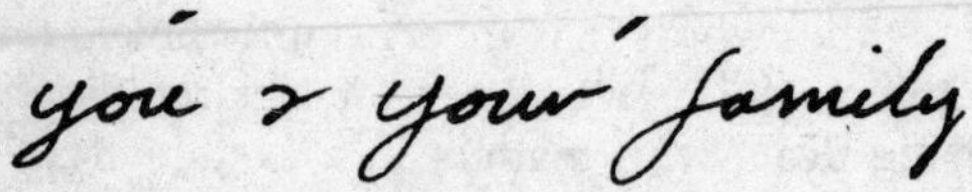

you & your family

Fig. 126

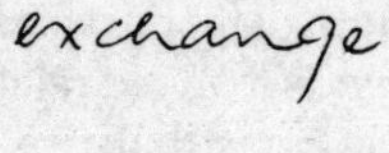

exchange

Fig. 127

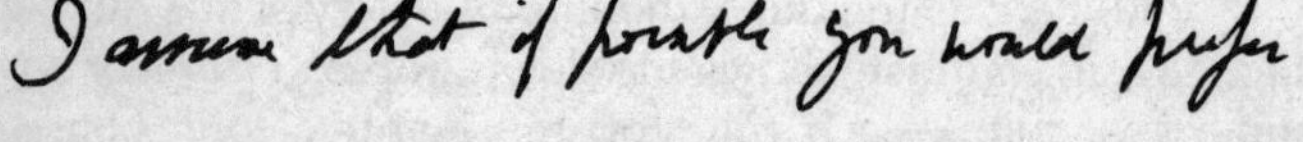

I assume that if possible you would prefer

Fig. 128

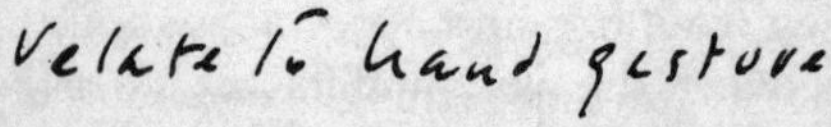

Velate to hand gestures

Fig. 129

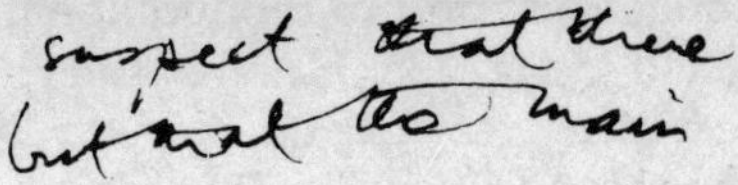

suspect that there

but not to main

Fig. 130

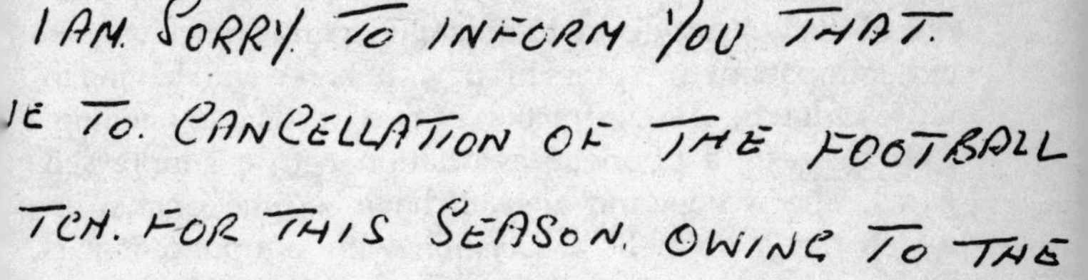

I AM. SORRY. TO INFORM YOU THAT.

E TO. CANCELLATION OF THE FOOTBALL

TCH. FOR THIS SEASON. OWING TO THE

Fig. 131

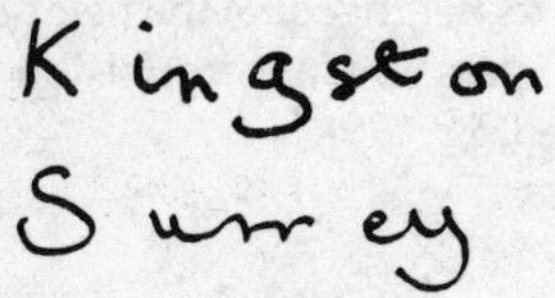

K i n g s t o n

S u r r e y

Fig. 132

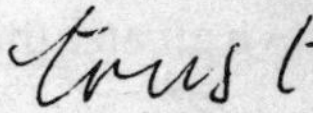

trust

Fig. 133

25 Disturbances

Some disturbances in handwriting can be readily understood, for example the correction of a spelling mistake or
the retracing of a faintly written word to make it legible. Fig.
134, however, shows a perfectly legible word which has
been retraced. It is possible that 'little' is a stimulus word
affecting the writer, creating in him an emotional response
and causing him to retrace it. It could also indicate the
writer's inability to leave things alone when finished:
desiring perfection, a neurotic uncertainty compels him to
retrace the word to improve it.

Stuttering, or any defect of speech, will cause disturbances in writing. The effort to produce the first letter of a word is reflected in Fig. 135. Having achieved the letter B the writer leaves a great gap (a recovery pause) before attempting the second letter. Fig. 136 shows marks made in the effort to get started.

Letters which are transposed within a word (Fig. 137) reveal the writer's desire to finish his writing quickly: he is either impatient to express his news or bored with having to write it down. The contraction of two words into one (Fig. 138) suggests a phonetic association with a suppressed word. The words 'and answer' have become 'ananswer' which has a phonetic association with 'announcer': it is reasonable to assume, therefore, that "announcer" is a stimulus word.

In adding to a letter, to make its height equal the height of other letters, the writer is expressing a compulsion to achieve greater things in his life (Fig. 139).

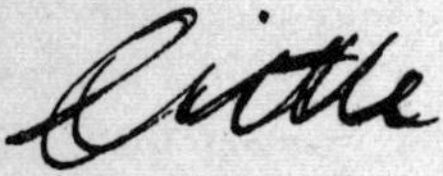

Fig. 134

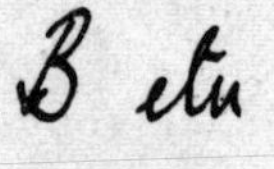

Fig. 135

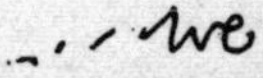

Fig. 136

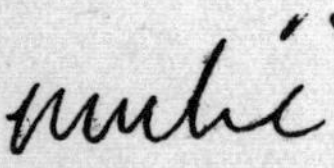

Fig. 137

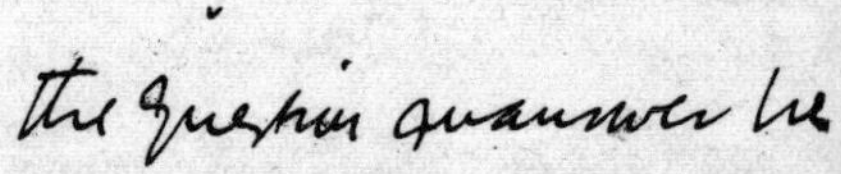

Fig. 138

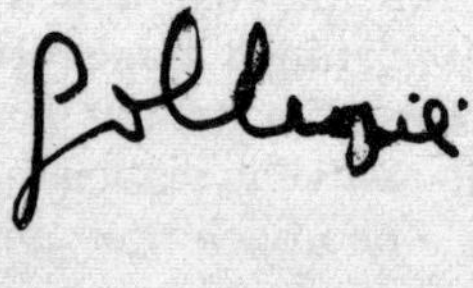

Fig. 139

26   Speed

HIGH SPEED

Writing done at high speed can be recognized by the following points: smooth strokes; no changes of direction of slant after a break; simplification; i dots become strokes or tent shapes; the left-hand margin tends to increase in width. Fig. 140 illustrates high speed which indicates spontaneous reactions, initiative and complete self-confidence.

LOW SPEED

Writing done at low speed can be recognized by the following points: lack of smoothness; occasional shaky loops; i dots precisely placed and dot-shaped; carefully written initial strokes; changes of direction after breaks; narrowing left-hand margin. Fig. 141 illustrates low speed which suggests a thoughtful, considerate disposition, self-consciousness and lack of originality and spontaneity.

REGULAR SPEED

A constant, regular speed (see Fig. 71) is used by characteristically well-organized and controlled people. Aroused emotions are easily detected in regular handwriting—a quickening of pace (impetuosity) or a slowing down of pace (unwillingness) will invariably disclose a stimulus word.

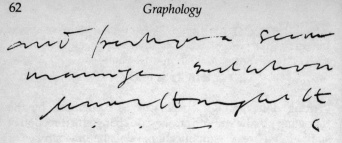

Fig. 140

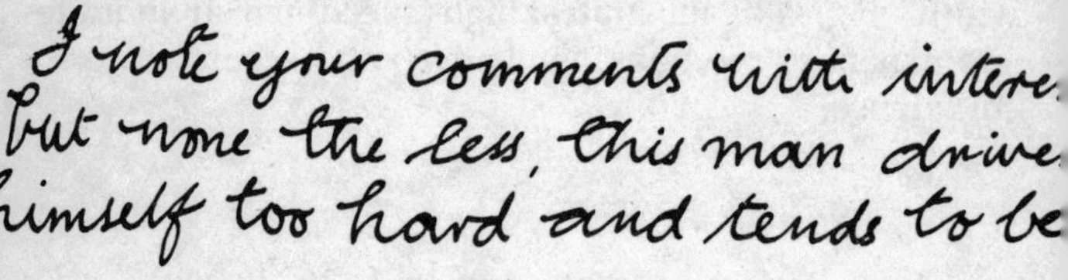

Fig. 141

27 Narrow Writing

Narrow writing (see Fig. 85) indicates reserve and a controlled, restricted social attitude: a mean streak and a
narrow-minded outlook give rise to intolerance, distrust
and acute self-consciousness. Narrow writing also suggests
steady concentration and a good sense of economy. The
narrower the writing the more intensified become the above
conditions. Fig. 142 shows how narrowness can cause
downstrokes to become covering strokes. The writer's
inhibitions become extreme to the point of avoiding all
social contact: he views everything with suspicion and
withdraws into seclusion. Fig. 143 shows narrow letters
with wide spacing between them. The wide spacing
indicates a free and easy attitude generally but the narrow
letters show that intimate relationships are affected by
inhibitions.

Tall, narrow writing (Fig. 144) reveals a self-possessed but inhibited person. Lack of imagination and an objectively critical nature make him unsociable.

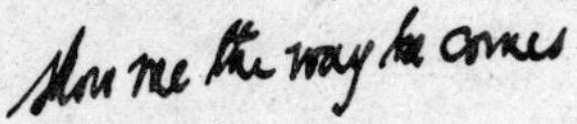

Fig. 142

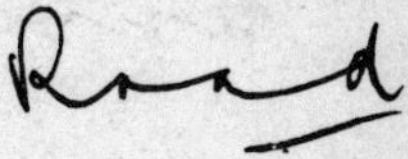

Fig. 143

Fig. 144

28 Wide Writing

Wide writing is expressive of the naturally expansive type (Fig. 145). He is characteristically self-indulgent, spontaneous and ego-bound: discipline, concentration and discretion are all thrown to the winds. Very wide writing (Fig. 146) reveals the interfering, immodest type who lacks any consideration for others.

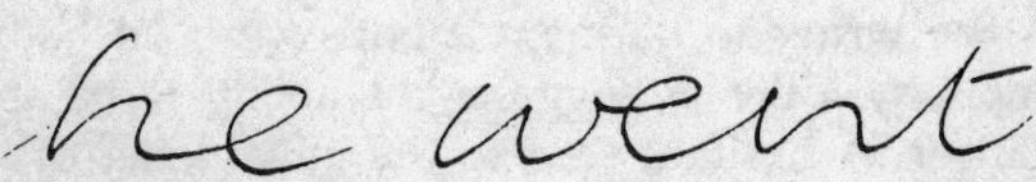

Fig. 145

Fig. 146

29   Initial Letters

The initial letter of each word reveals the writer's intended social attitude.

An introductory stroke, as in Fig. 147, indicates the slow thinker: he mulls over matters which he would prefer to postpone. Arcade (covering) introductory strokes (Fig. 148) show that the writer resents interference. Garland introductory strokes (Fig. 149) reveal an ingratiating attitude. The line curving upwards from beneath the initial letter in Fig. 150 is an emphatic gesture representing eloquence. The long lead-in stroke on the initial letter in Fig. 151 reveals an aggressive excitable nature full of fight and provocation: the writer will go through unnecessary preliminaries before dealing with any main issue.

There are no strokes or flourishes on the initial letters in Fig. 152: the writer is a quick thinker who gets things done in an original and direct way. The concentrated start in Fig. 153 reveals the writer to be intense but controlled both mentally and physically: it suggests the ability to be an excellent dancer. A hesitant start to the initial letter of a word (Fig. 154) indicates that everything new (relationships, work), is met with a temporary indecisiveness.

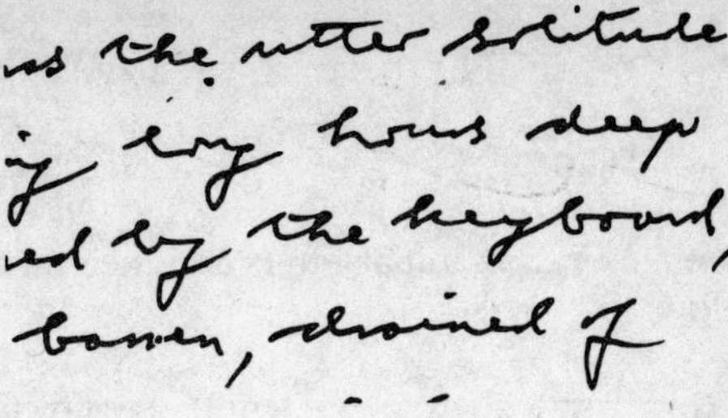

as the utter solitude
of every house deep
ed by the keyboard,
barren, drained of

Fig. 147

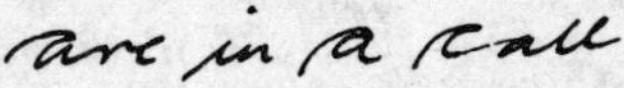

are in a call

Fig. 148

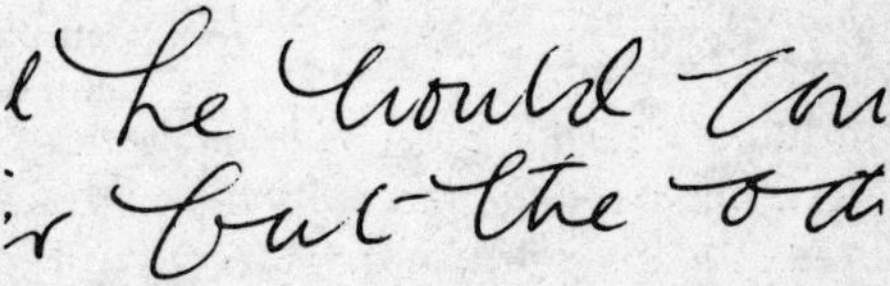

l he would con
r but the oth

Fig. 149

Fig. 150

Fig. 151

Thank you for your le
I will ask member

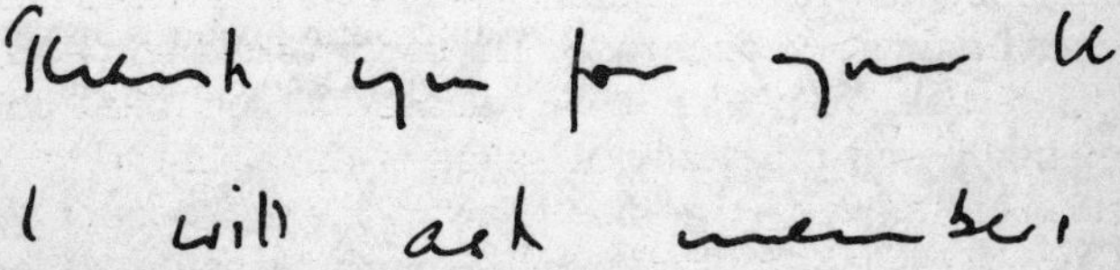

Fig. 152

Fig. 153 Fig. 154

Some other kinds of initial letters and their meanings are given below.

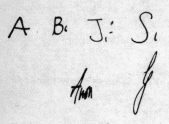

(script) constructive mind, methodical, reliable

(narrow) shyness

(extending stroke) self-importance

(an introductory curve) maternal/ paternal instinct

(top and bottom of equal length) intense concentration, determination and will-power

(stroke covering word) instinctively protective and patronizing

(curving stroke) responsibility

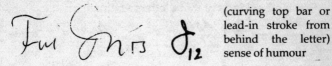

(disconnected) a strong imagination and a fund of ideas but lacking the ability to put them to advantage

(curving top bar or lead-in stroke from behind the letter) sense of humour

(long lead-in from above) enterprise

30 Final Letters

The final letter reveals the writer's natural social qualities.

A well-proportioned final letter (Fig. 155) reveals a wholly trustworthy person who is practical and self-sufficient: he is very good at assessing people and is not easily deceived. A neglected or illegible last letter (Fig. 156) indicates unreliability and untrustworthiness. A very large final letter (Fig. 157) is indicative of risky impulses and points to an inclination to fulfil fantasies. The extension of a final letter to the edge of the paper (Fig. 158) signifies the writer's distrust of others causing him to take elaborate security measures with his property.

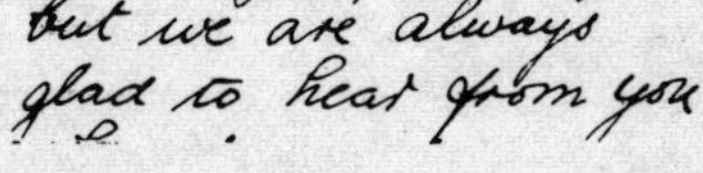

here day after day,
but we are always
glad to hear from you

Fig. 155

I don't want the 6

Fig. 156

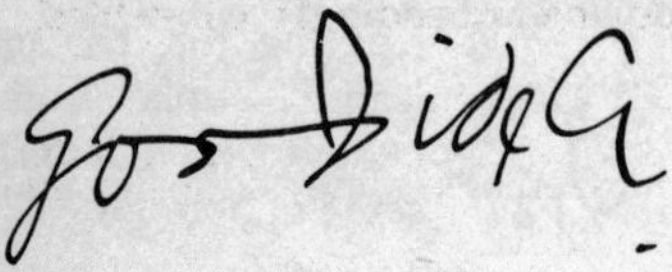

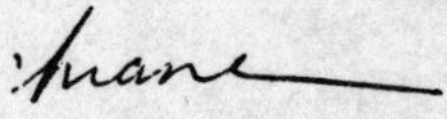

Fig. 157

Fig. 158

Some other kinds of final letters and their meanings are given below:

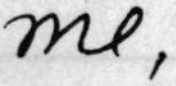

me,	(abrupt ending) self-discipline, determination, selfishness
ton the	(heavy stroke ending to right) aggression and obstinacy
;th	(downwards and to the right) reticent and inclined to be selfish
sue	(slight curve upwards) generous
time.	(higher curve) self-conscious
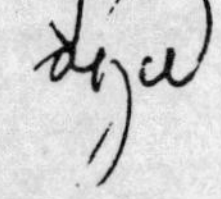	(curving backwards to cover the letter) not entirely truthful

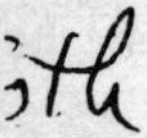

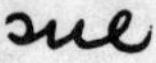

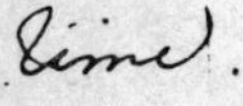

(ending in heavy downward stroke) dogmatic, opinionated, obstinate

(light downward ending) weak-willed

(long horizontal ending) curiosity and determination

(long rising ending) daring—will try anything once

(the last downstroke is not completed) will never give a straightforward answer

(finishing with an extra curve) pays attention to detail

(ending in a point) purposeful

31 Diminishing and Expanding

Diminishing words in a normal size of handwriting (Fig. 159) are a sure sign of maturity and diplomacy. The smaller the writing the more psychologically effective is the writer's strategy.

Expanding writing (Fig. 160) reveals a childish impetuosity and a limited social comprehension: in cultured handwriting it denotes lack of diplomacy.

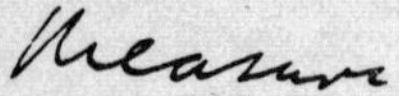

Fig. 159 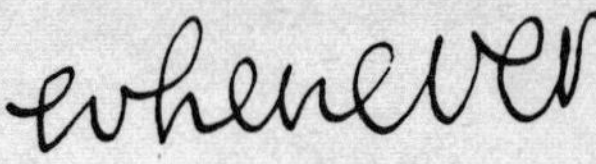   Fig. 160

32   Capitals

A high, large capital (Fig. 161) signifies pride, self-confidence and independence: it is expressive of a feeling of superiority. It could, however, indicate a dreamlike quality with religious overtones if there is a supporting dominant upper zone. Fig. 162 shows diminished capitals which denote modesty but they could also be a gesture of disparagement towards the addressee, in which case the writer's signature would be comparatively larger. The enlarging of small letters to make capitals (Fig. 163) reveals respect and affection. A lower case letter substituting a capital letter (Fig. 164) reveals a disregard for convention. In the case of the letter I (the symbol for ego), where a lower case letter substitutes the capital (Fig. 165), the writer is revealing self-devaluation. The enclosing of a second letter by a capital (Fig. 166) denotes secrecy. Capitals that reach into the lower zone indicate the psychologist (Fig. 167): the writer has a deep understanding of the creative and mystical qualities in Man.

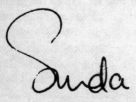

Fig. 161 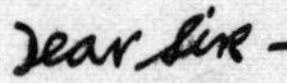   Fig. 162

Fig. 163 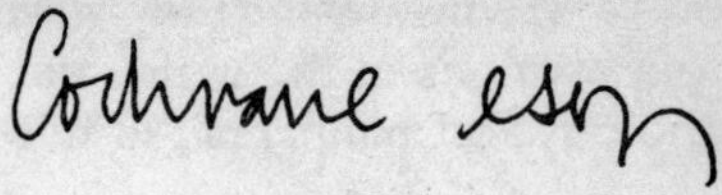 *Fig. 164*

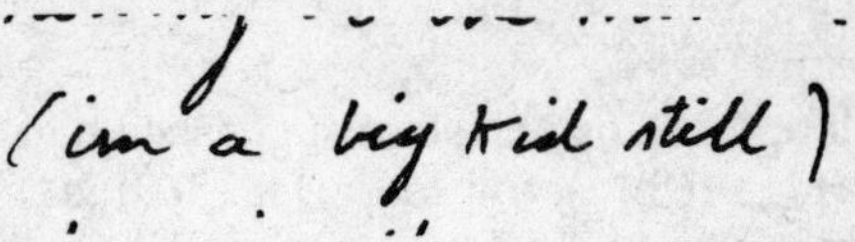

Fig. 165

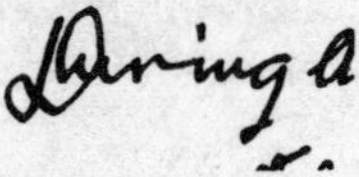

Fig. 166

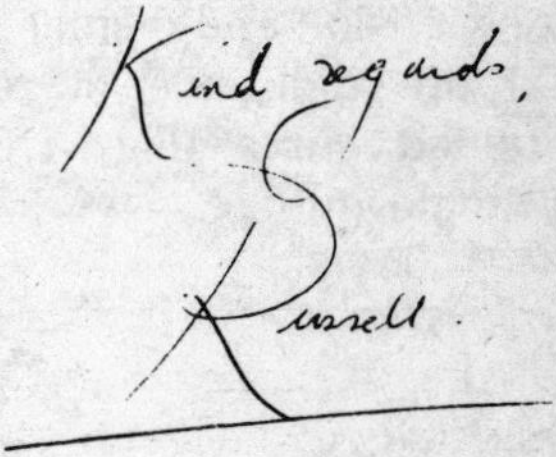

Fig. 167

33 Loops

A loop is made from two movements: in the case of a lower zone loop a downward stroke is effected by the flexor muscles to a point where a reflex action (inhibition) prevents further descent. The stroke then turns upward in response to a counter-directive impulse, the movement being effected by the extensor muscles. In the case of an upper zone loop an upward stroke is effected by the extensor muscles to a point where an inhibitive reflex action prevents further ascent; the stroke then turns downwards in response to a counter-directive impulse, the movement being effected by the flexor muscles. The length and quality of the downward and upward strokes are controlled by the reflex actions of the writer and correspond to the mental and physical manner of the individual.

UPPER LOOPS ·

A small loop high on the stem suggests a narrow-minded attitude (Fig. 168). A full loop (Fig. 169) is made by the emotional person who has a natural love for music and singing. Stunted loops (Fig. 170) indicate modesty and a lack of imagination. Very shaky loops (Fig. 171) reveal an inner tension and mental fatigue. Compressed loops (Fig. 172) are indicative of repressions and inhibitions. A flattened curve (Fig. 173) reveals an aggressive and obstinate attitude.

Fig. 168 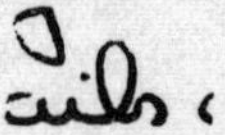   Fig. 169    Fig. 170

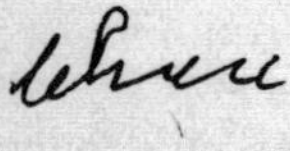

Fig. 171 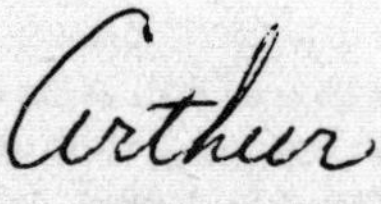   Fig. 172 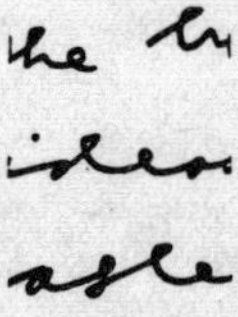   Fig. 173

LOWER LOOPS

Wide loops to the left (Fig. 174) form a regressive movement; the writer is always relating to the past in which the Mother was important. Wide loops to the right (Fig. 175) reflect a progressive instinct. The flowing full loop in Fig. 176, done in heavy pressure, is made by warm, generous people who are physically strong and sexually impulsive: they have a developed sense of colour and rhythm and are graceful dancers. A truncated loop (Fig. 177) reveals reticence (the upward stroke is suddenly stopped, i.e. inhibited): clannish instincts cause the writer to be very involved with his family. Loops filled with ink (Fig. 178) are the result of the sensual and artistic feelings of the writer. In Fig. 179 the loop has been reduced to a tight circle, the mark of the loner. A rightward stroke extending from the circle (Fig. 180) is a 'feeler' for reassurance and depicts insecurity. An aggressive nature is revealed by loops ending in a heavy downward thrust (Fig. 181). The writer who makes very long loops (Fig. 182) does not recognize his limitations, uses up all resources of energy and becomes moody and irresolute.

Two loops (Fig. 183) point to eccentricity: the writer, vain and neurotically compulsive, has strange individualistic habits and odd ideas. An unduly large, open loop (Fig. 184) indicates the extravert for whom money has great importance. In Fig. 185 the slant of the loop is in opposition to the slant of the rest of the writing: in heavy pressure it points to the writer having a resistance to sexual intercourse; in light pressure it denotes marked lapses in physical energies. Very short loops (Fig. 186) could be indicative of injury to the legs or feet but usually represent an apprehensive approach to sexual matters. When the loop forms a triangle with a horizontal baseline (Fig. 187) the writer is emphasizing his interest in materialism.

Fig. 174   Fig. 175

Fig. 176

Fig. 177

Fig. 178

Fig. 179

Fig. 180

Fig. 181

Fig. 182

Fig. 183

Fig. 184

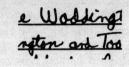

Fig. 185   Fig. 186   Fig. 187

34 Hooks

Hooks are unconscious expressions of compulsive urges.

The tick hook (Fig. 188) reveals an acquisitive nature. The horizontal hook (Fig. 189) is indicative of a searching, probing mind. The back hook in Fig. 190 reflects possessiveness. A t bar with both ends hooked (Fig. 191) signifies a neurotic compulsion to be always doing something.

Fig. 188   Fig. 189

Fig. 190   Fig. 191

35 Strokes

Rightward strokes following g and y (Fig. 192) reveal a generous and sympathetic interest in people: if the strokes extend into the upper zone they express a sarcastic attitude. A downward stroke with no loop or hook (Fig. 193) shows concentration and good mathematical ability: in dealing with people the writer likes to get straight to the point. The same stroke in a truncated form (Fig. 194) reveals physical weakness and, in a needlelike fashion (Fig. 195), a sarcastic tongue and quick temper. A leftward convex stroke (Fig. 196) reveals a covetous quality, the writer often making unreasonable demands. Long, weak downstrokes (Fig. 197) suggest that the writer dwells on his shortcomings and that his thoughts turn easily to suicide. Backward strokes (Fig. 198) are always a sign of introversion: those which curve forwards (Fig. 199) reflect an obedient nature and can be taken as a gesture of respect. An outward, diagonal stroke from the middle zone to the lower zone (Fig. 200) is found in the handwriting of those who prefer to stay silent in an emotional argument.

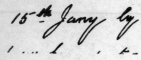

Fig. 192   Fig. 193   Fig. 194

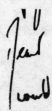

Fig. 195   Fig. 196   Fig. 197

Fig. 198   Fig. 199   Fig. 200

CONCEALING STROKES

Concealing strokes, i.e. upward and downward strokes
which do not form loops but overlap each other, imply
constraint or secrecy.

In the upper zone (intellectuality) concealing strokes tell
us that the writer's thoughts are private (Fig. 201). In the
middle zone (emotion) the example (Fig. 202) shows the
word 'request' in which the two e's are blocked: the writer is
unable to express his feelings clearly, resulting in frequent
bouts of silence. In the lower zone (instinct) concealing
strokes reveal a suppression of physical drives and
impulses (Fig. 203).

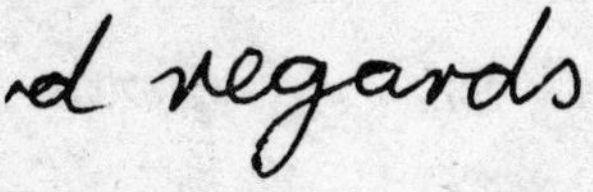

Fig. 201 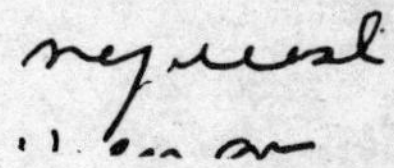   Fig. 202 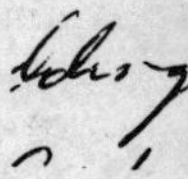   Fig. 203

COVERING STROKES

Covering strokes (Fig. 204) are a deliberate tracing of letters
during which the pen is never lifted from the paper: they
reveal caution and a methodical thought process.

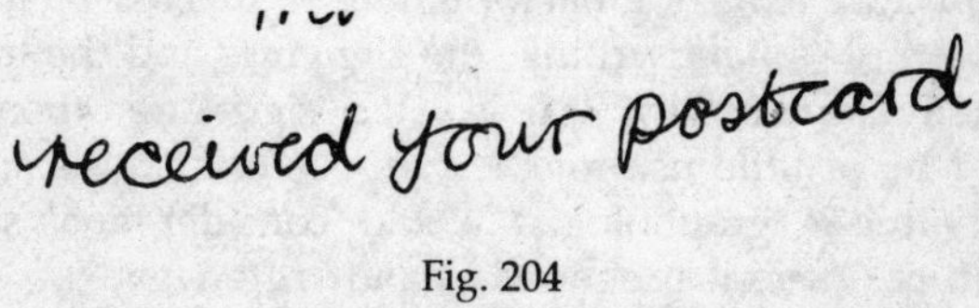

Fig. 204

COUNTER-STROKES

Counter-strokes indicate strong opposition to conventional

rules and reveal propensities for stealing, fraud and lying:
they are the mark of the bluff, bragging type of person.

In Fig. 205 the word 'wind' begins with a counter-arcade
w in a garland connective form. Fig. 206 shows the word
'man' written in an arcade connective form but the a is a
counter-garland. In Fig. 207 the capital S terminates with a
counter-downstroke instead of the natural upward con-
tinuation. In Fig. 208 the e ending is a counter-left-stroke
instead of the normal right extension.

| Fig. 205 | Fig. 206 | Fig. 207 | Fig. 208 |

36   The Signature

One of the first words a child is taught to write is his name.
Writing the name over and over again creates an emotional
involvement with it which is retained throughout life.
Consequently, while a person's handwriting alters with the
development of character, his signature will invariably
remain close to its original form. It is for this reason that, in
most people's handwriting, the signature and the text do
not tally structurally. An isolated signature, therefore,
would be of little use for the purpose of analysis and no
conscientious graphologist would consider analysing a
signature unless it appended a handwritten text.

People who are very much in the public's eye often create
special signatures: entertainers, sportsmen, politicians, and
so on develop a flamboyant style as an unconscious
expression of ego; millionaires, property owners, etc.,
develop a mass of complicated strokes and embellishments

designed, they hope, to prevent imitation. It is a fact, however, that involved constructions are fairly easy to imitate—it is the simple, natural curve that proves to be inimitable.

A legible signature (Fig. 209) reflects sincerity. An illegible signature (Fig. 210) reveals unreliability and evasiveness but a signature which is illegible because of its complicated structure (Fig. 211) points to a complex and interesting personality.

A signature written in the size and style of the text reveals a continuing expression of modesty and sincerity in private and public life. Written smaller than the text it is indicative of unconscious self-devaluation: in both cases a negative personality is revealed. Written larger than the text it becomes the mark of the autocrat.

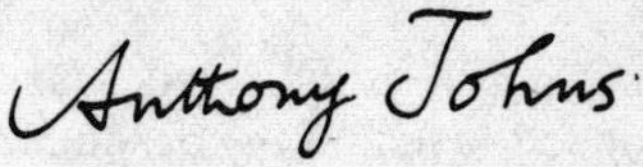

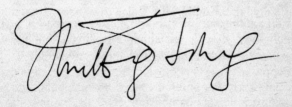

Fig. 209

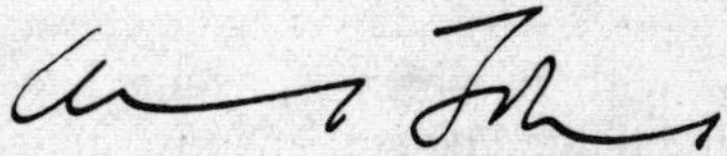

Fig. 210

Fig. 211

THE FIRST NAME

People who emphasize the first letter of their first name are usually unconsciously relating their name to a very happy childhood when the first name was constantly used and the surname was unimportant. A woman, unhappy in marriage and resenting the married name, will unconsciously emphasize the first letter of her first name and either diminish the size of the married name or drop it altogether.

Conscious emphasis is made by those who like familiarity and have a desire to be on first-name terms with everybody; they, also, may drop the surname. A modest person with a famous surname may consciously emphasize his first name in an endeavour to tone down the attraction of his surname—an independent streak may banish the surname altogether.

A first name which is enlarged and embellished is characteristic of self-love and the desire for approval from others. It can also be a deliberate demonstration of 'this is my name' by those who are fearful of a childhood nickname carrying on into adulthood.

THE SURNAME

Pride in the surname is indicated by emphasis of the initial letter. Over-emphasis of the surname reveals a sense of prestige gained from the name.

A signature that incorporates all the names of a person reveals snobbery. A signature consisting of initials and surname indicates a person's disapproval of familiarity.

DOTS WITH SIGNATURES

A dot forming the beginning of a signature (Fig. 212)

denotes a pause while the writer concentrates on the construction of his name: such a person will deliberately build up an intensity of expression before dynamically releasing it. A dot appearing at the end of a signature (Fig. 213) means that the writer considers his word to be final. A colon at the end of a signature (Fig. 214) is an instinctive mark revealing an urge to say more but deciding not to.

Fig. 212   Fig. 213   Fig. 214

STROKES ATTACHED TO SIGNATURES

Flourishes on signatures recreate the scribble formation made in early childhood and, therefore, express unconscious emotional feelings.

Extending to the right horizontally, the stroke signifies a defensive attitude (Fig. 215). Sharply angled to the upper zone it reveals an aggressive streak (Fig. 216) but, gently curving to the upper zone, it represents generosity (Fig. 217). A stroke which returns cutting through the name reveals suicidal tendencies (Fig. 218). An end stroke made up of several curves (Fig. 219) reveals the exhibitionist but jagged lines (Fig. 220) indicate a sense of compulsion and determination. People who suffer from anxiety tend to put up barriers and become unapproachable; thus an end stroke which encircles the signature signifies an anxiety state (Fig. 221). The last letter ending in a sudden curving movement emphasizes a forceful personality (Fig. 222) but an involved flourish (Fig. 223) is expressive of the desire to feel important and is, therefore, a compensation for inferiority.

A. g. Neal

Fig. 215

A. g. Neal

Fig. 216

A. g. Neal

Fig. 217

Fig. 218

Fig. 219

Fig. 220

Fig. 221

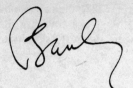

Fig. 222   Fig. 223

THE SIGNATURE IN RELATION TO THE TEXT

Placed centrally   natural modesty, caution and a desire for
                     security.
Extreme right   eagerly active and impatient.
Left   retiring instincts; a tendency to withdraw
                     from society.
Extreme left   indicative of an anxiety state; a strong
                     inclination to escape reality; possibly
                     suicidal.
Close to text   feels a strong bond with the content of
                     the text.
Far from text   detached from the subject matter
                     whether consciously or unconsciously.

THE PARAPH

All marks and flourishes under a signature are compensation for an inferiority complex; many are defence mechanisms against the addressee. Signatures without paraphs are written by natural, modest and discriminating people. A forward and backward stroke (Fig. 224) suggests a dramatic instinct. A short, simple line (Fig. 225) denotes an impressive personality. A straight line continuing the length of the signature emphasizes the ego (Fig. 226); if the line is very heavy an assertive personality is indicated. Self-confidence is depicted by a small convex line (Fig. 227); persistence by over and under strokes (Fig. 228). A stroke covering the whole of the signature expresses the desire to dominate (Fig. 229).

Fig. 224

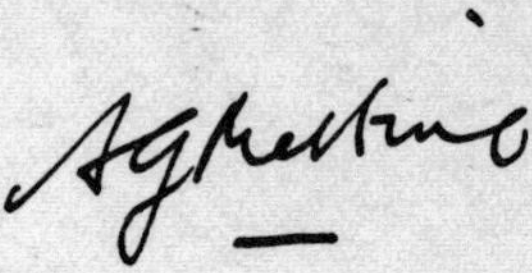

Fig. 225

Fig. 226

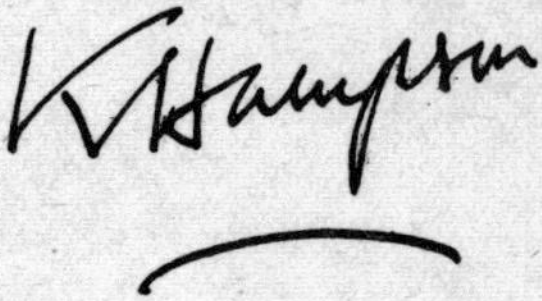

Fig. 227

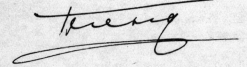

Fig. 228

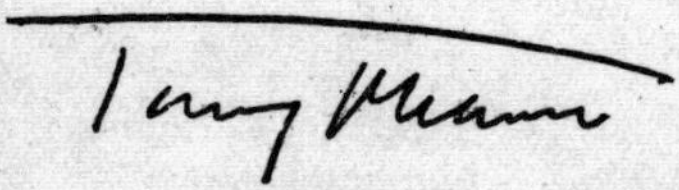

Fig. 229

37   The Alphabet

Individual letters in a person's handwriting will reveal particular characteristics. The same structural deviation from the copybook style is often found in different letters, as shown below. A deviation must occur frequently and certainly more than four times in a handwriting to be acknowledged as a positive characteristic trait.

(closed letters) caution, diplomacy, good business ability, loyalty

(open letters) talkative, frank, submissive, untrustworthy with secrets

(knotted) tenacious, thorough

(copybook) modesty, gullibility, trust

(elaborate curves) egoism

(script) constructive thought, cultured, high intelligence

(pointed loops) resentful attitude

(curling end stroke) imagination, poetic qualities

(square formation) interest in construction and mechanics

INDIVIDUAL STRUCTURES

A.   (double loop) secretive

(downstroke crossbar) disappointment

(low crossing) inferiority

B. (larger lower curve) generosity

(larger upper curve) caution, doubt, cynicism

C.   (double stroke inside curve) calculating

D. 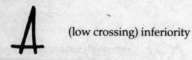   (curving top endings) cultured, imaginative

   (downstroke to right) taciturn

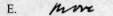 (downstroke separated) talkative

E.  (resembles i) mental keenness

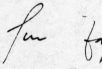 (casually looped) thoughtless, casual

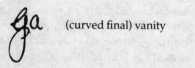 (Greek formation) cultured, quick, clever

F. (flowing curves) fluent thought process

 (top or bottom only looped) common sense, good judgement, gets straight to the point

G. (like an 8) very adaptable and optimistic; takes things in his stride and prefers to learn from experience

 (capital like an 8) cultured

(curved final) vanity

H.

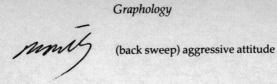

(back sweep) aggressive attitude

(loop crossing) solves problems by logic and strategy

I. The capital I = Ego. The ego is the influential mechanism of the reality process: it is the mediator between the person and reality and its main function is the perception of reality and adaptation to it.

English is the only language in which the symbol for ego stands alone. The construction, size and position of the capital I, in relation to other words, are of great importance in analysis.

SIZE

If the I and other capitals are equal in size the ego can be considered equable. If the I is more elaborate than other capitals it reveals a pronounced self-consciousness. If the I fluctuates in size the ego is unsteady.

THE DISTANCE BETWEEN I AND OTHER WORDS

If there are large spaces between the I and other words the writer prefers isolation to company. If the I is very close to a preceding or following word the writer fears being alone and craves company all the time. If the distance between the I and other words fluctuates social behaviour fluctuates.

Any amendments to the I reveal doubts about the ego.

(solitary stroke) a straightforward approach to all things

 (top and bottom bars) constructive, practical and businesslike

 (closed loop) self-esteem and confidence

 (slanting to left) introverted and lacking in confidence. In an upright or right-slanting writing it reveals a guilt complex.

 (beginning at the bottom) a counter-stroke: a sign of the rebel

 (introductory stroke from the right) humorous and talkative

 (large loop) vanity

 (huge loop) megalomania

(reaching into upper zone) a contemplative type

The placement and shape of the dot over the small i is important

 (c shape) a good observer

 (comma shape) prone to anxiety states

(behind the i) procrastination

(directly over the i) orderly and exact; a perfectionist

(directly over and very close) the writer exercises precision and accuracy and has an excellent memory. If the dot is in heavy pressure the writer is concerned with detail. It also depicts materialism and lack of imagination.

(no dot) careless and likely to be unreliable

(dot beyond i) enthusiastic and impulsive

nior clin (vertical and horizontal dashes) witty, humorous and diplomatic

himself (tent-shaped) a discriminating person with a highly-developed faculty of observation; possessing a cutting sense of humour

triumph, having (high up) a very strong imagination evolving into fantasies

links with Graphol. eciate your birth details (circle dots) the non-conformist; has creative skills but lacks definite aims. In the example the i in 'details' has the conventional dot indicating that the circle dot is an affectation expressing a desire for attention.

expressing feels (joining the i dot to a following letter or word) bases conclusion on observation and reason

Directors (the i dot is incorporated in a continuous stroke, the pen not being lifted from the paper). Indicative of inconsistency and a tendency to become embroiled in arguments.

K. *Cork* (like an R) defiance

L.  (large base loop) vanity and a desire for money

M. **my** (rounded tops) immature, submissive and very obedient. Not an adaptable person

 (angular tops, rounded bottoms) a penetrating mind and yielding emotions create many mental struggles.

 (top and bottom angular) intolerant and unyielding

 (first top angle higher than others) self-assured, ambitious and independent

 (final top angle higher than others) an assumed authority compensates for discontent and unfulfilment. Self-conscious and quarrelsome.

(trident M) artistic, creative

(capital rounded top) a modest, natural person who is never given to pretensions.

(spiralled) vanity

O.   *tos*   (two loops) deceitful

Loin   (one loop) secretive

London   (alternate open and closed) forthright and plain speaking

ndon Tooth   (casual flowing formation) will always avoid unnecessary effort

(coiled) sense of humour

P.   *zeffin*   (open) compliant nature

Slish   (upstroke parted from stem) aggressive and sarcastic

Peter   (wide rhythmic loop) thrives on physical activity

R.   (flat-topped) strong visual sense, curious and observant

Cork Garde   (simplified) a lively cultured mind; enthusiastic

Graphology

Paul (formless) deceitful

afar (reaching to upper zone) likes to be noticed

Arthur (looped) prejudiced

inform (capital within a word) given to pretensions

MR. (short, raised stroke) ambition
ARTH.

S. *usey* (equally looped) expansive but ineffective

Su (high loop) does not invite intimacy

Sat (elongated) likes to keep on the move

T. Study of the placement, shape and degree of pressure
    of the t cross stroke is of great value in analysis. There
    are as many as 72 types of cross-stroke (t bar) some of
    which are given below:

(script) well-balanced and dependable

(rising above stem) enthusiastic, impulsive and ambitious but too hasty to be thorough.

(left of the stem) indecisive and lacking will-power. A sign of repression and dependency. If repeated many times the writer is expressing guilt feelings which cause a lowering of self-esteem and consequent acute depression. In a child's handwriting it indicates that too many decisions are made for him.

(thickening bar) possessing a temper which builds up to a rage

(diminishing in thickness) a quick temper which suddenly dies

(the bar is above the stem) an adventurous disposition and a strong imagination. Good judgement and foresight. In a child's hand-writing it indicates a vivid imagination. Heavy pressure signifies a love of physical adventure—mountaineering, etc.; light pressure indicates an adventurous mentality, the desire to explore and to learn from experience.

(a very heavy t bar pointing downwards) the sign of the aggressor. A strongly opinionated, dominating person always ready for an argument or a fight.

(concave) irresponsible. If the bar is lighter than the rest of the handwriting the writer is weak-willed; if the bar is placed low on the stem the writer will look for an easy way out of situations.

 (convex) the mark of self-control. If continually repeated it reflects a perpetual self-control. In the centre of the stem it denotes very good physical and mental co-ordination. If it lies above the stem the writer has a strong imagination and mystical tendencies.

 (resting on the top of the stem) a perfectionist

 (a long bar from the top of the stem) domineering and very ambitious

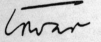 (wavy) good-humoured and full of fun

(rightward bar not attached to the stem) very enthusiastic and impatient

(no bar) very easily affected by sensations. A spontaneous liar.

 (a loop above the stem) eccentricity in dress and home decorations

(the rising stroke and stem both crossed) inscrutable

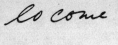 (no bar: resembling the letter l) being friendly to people is an automatic, routine and superficial business.

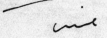 (a simplified stem without bar) absent-minded and careless. Indicative of repressions, i.e. banishing from the conscious ideas or impulses that are unacceptable to it.

 (the bar without the stem) enjoys being perverse

X. (cross) likes to be accurate

expe (copybook) does not easily adjust to situations; talkative.

38　Standards of Writing

Standard 1　A natural, rhythmic, original style with good spacing (Fig. 230)

Standard 2　Curved forms, good spacing, pastose (Fig. 231)

Standard 3　Naturally large writing, even pressure, reasonable spacing (Fig. 232)

Standard 4　Copybook, limited originality, slow (Fig. 233)

Standard 5　A natural, unimaginative hand, strong variation, tending towards illegibility (Fig. 234)

Standard 6　An obvious attempt to create an impression (Fig. 235)

Standard 7　Erratic spacing, negative deviations (Fig. 236)

Standard 8　Ill-mannered (Fig. 237)

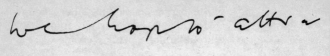
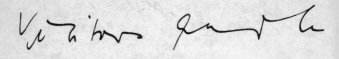
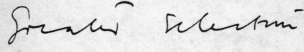
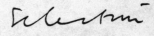

Fig. 230

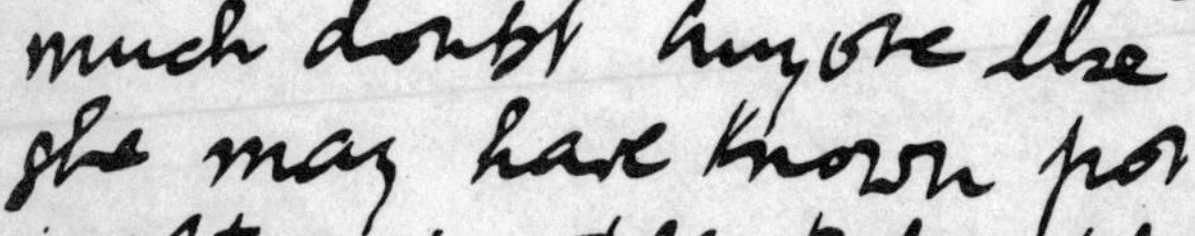

much doubt anyone else
she may have known por
inobtrusive tell-tale idi

Fig. 231

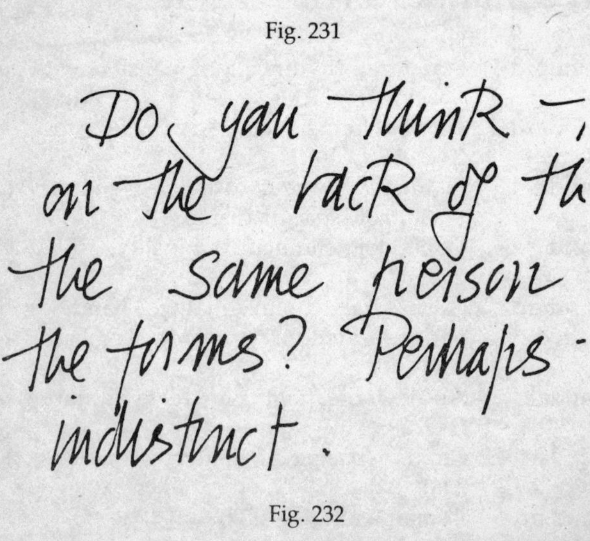

Do you think —,
on the back of th
the same person
the forms? Perhaps -
indistinct.

Fig. 232

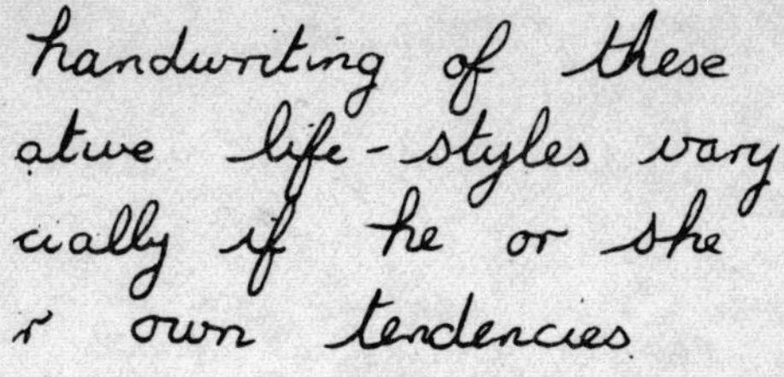

handwriting of these
ative life-styles vary
cially if he or she
r own tendencies

Fig. 233

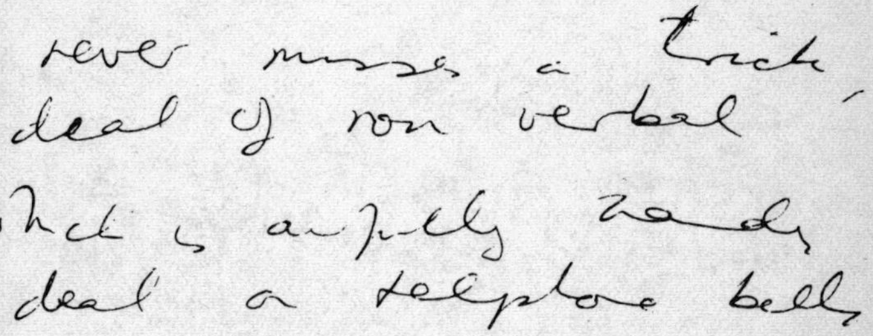

sever misses a trick,
deal of non verbal

which is awfully handy,
deal a telephone bell,

Fig. 234

it and if

involve on a

intending to

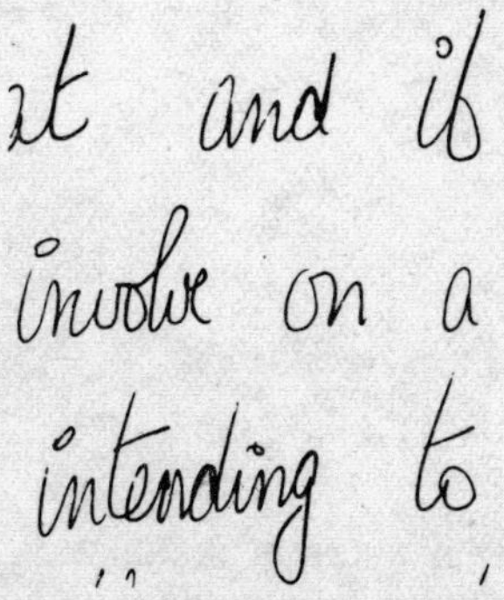

Fig. 235

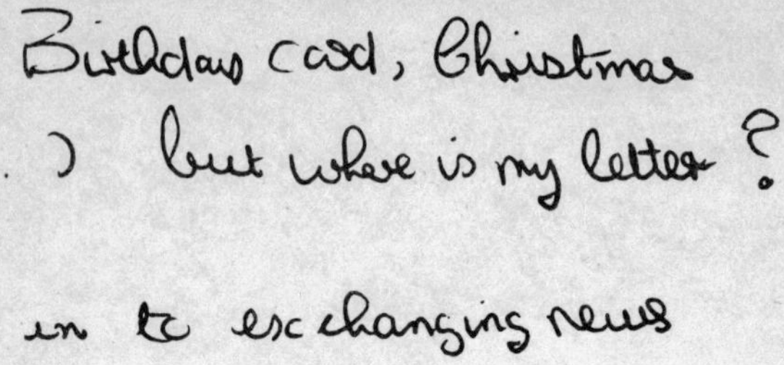

Birthday card, Christmas

) but where is my letter?

in to exchanging news

Fig. 236

Fig. 237

39 Dominant and Counter-Dominant

When a recurring single trait dominates a handwriting it becomes the governing psychological factor in a character analysis.

The over-emphasized t bars in Fig. 238 reveal a pre-occupation with ideas and aspirations; they dominate the handwriting and signify a characteristic desire to escape the realities of life.

One feature in a handwriting may be dramatically prominent because of its contrast with the general writing form. In Fig. 239 the leftward endings in a right-tending handwriting are counter-dominant and reveal strong opposition to normally accepted rules. A counter-dominant is important in analysis because it reveals a basic characteristic which is not normally apparent.

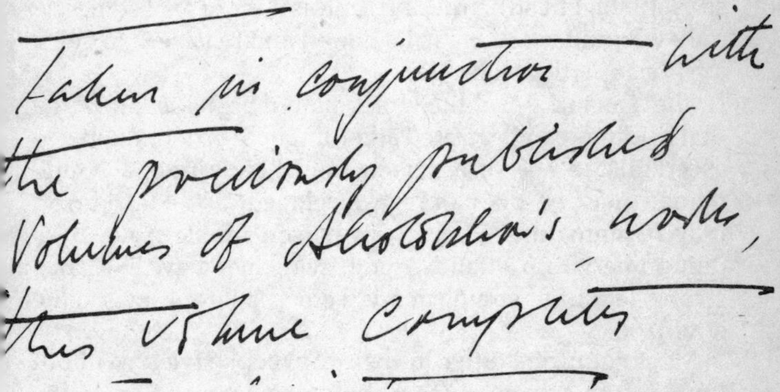

Fig. 238

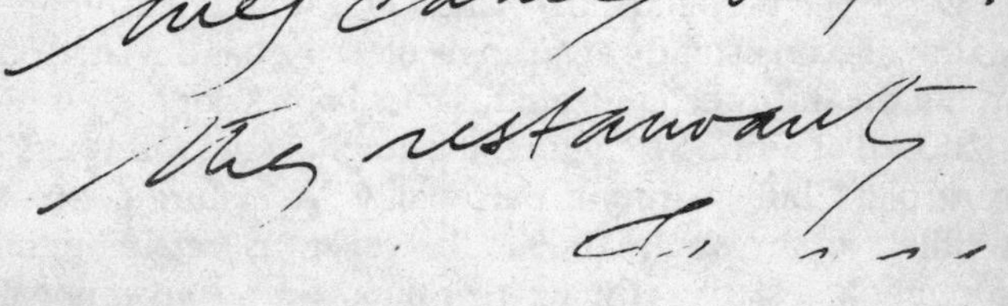

Fig. 239

40 Analysis

The graphologist should be supplied with as much writing, on unlined paper, as possible: several sheets of a letter would be ideal. Writing that is done especially for analysis is not suitable: an inevitable element of self-consciousness would affect important formations such as t bars, i dots and loops.

A character analysis should never take less than two days: it can often take longer. Time should be allowed for reflection: there are many details, some contradictory, which have to be related to form a pertinent, comprehensive, intelligent structure and, unless it is a case of someone only wanting to know "Is he honest and reliable?", a quick job is a superficial job.

The age and sex of the writer should be made known so that findings can be related accordingly. It is not possible to ascertain the age of a person from his writing: a young person may be prematurely developed, an older person may be immature. Similarly, a person's sex can never be determined from a handwriting: many men have in them a strong feminine strain, many women a strong masculine strain.

Most countries differ in their copybook styles. Without knowing in which country the writer learnt to write the graphologist cannot assess deviations from the appropriate copybook style. For example, Americans are taught to write at an angle of 80° (see Fig. 88): English and Dutch people are taught to write at an angle of 60°: German people are taught to write in a perpendicular hand (90°). If an Englishman's writing is consistently at an angle of 90° he has deviated 30° in a leftward direction from his copybook slant and, if his standard of writing is mature, the graphologist will assess a controlled but charming personality. A mature German writing at an angle of 90°, however, is retaining his copybook slant thus revealing a conventional, unimaginative personality.

Many graphologists use worksheets which are usually designed to suit the individual's working method: their use lies mainly in clarifying details and allowing a quick assessment of the client's intelligence. For example, Fig. 240 shows the worksheet relating to the letter reproduced in Fig. 241 and, in the graph section, it can be seen that legibility, layout, spacing, co-ordination, i dots and t bars are rated highly and that simplification and general standard of writing are very good. The graphologist, therefore, knows at a glance that he is dealing with a highly intelligent, well-balanced boy and will view all other details within the framework of that knowledge.

Of great importance to the graphologist are the protractor, to determine the correct degree of slant, and the magnifying glass which is essential for scrutiny of stroke endings, breaks and amendments.

ADVERSE INFLUENCES

Analysis should not be attempted

if the writing is on greasy paper. The ink will not consistently adhere to the surface.

if the writing is on porous paper. The ink will spread and obliterate line thicknesses or fill open loops.

if the writing has been done with a ball-point pen. The ink-flow will fluctuate and will invariably make blobs.

if the writing has been done on a very small piece of paper.

if the writing paper has been resting on an uneven or rough surface.

if the writing has been done under unusual conditions such as extreme cold; in a moving vehicle; while experiencing an extreme emotion.

if the sample, is, in fact, a photograph or a photostat or any form of reproduction.

A conscientious graphologist would not consider a

sample of handwriting which reflected any of the above conditions.

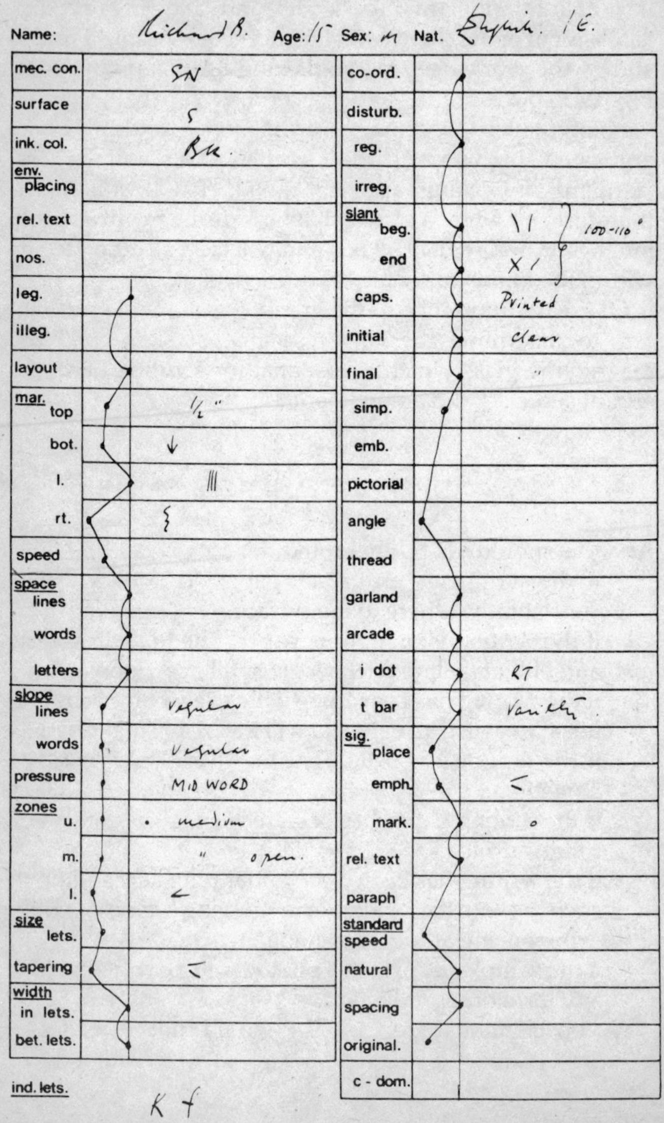

Name:	*Richard B.*	Age: *15*	Sex: *M*	Nat. *English. / E.*

mec. con.	SN	co-ord.		
surface	S	disturb.		
ink. col.	Bu.	reg.		
env. placing		irreg.		
rel. text		slant beg.	| |	100-110°
nos.		end	× /	
leg.		caps.		Printed
illeg.		initial		clear
layout		final		''
mar. top	½"	simp.		
bot.	↓	emb.		
l.	///	pictorial		
rt.	{	angle		
speed		thread		
space lines		garland		
words		arcade		
letters		i dot		RT
slope lines	Regular	t bar		Variety
words	Regular	sig. place		
pressure	MID WORD	emph.		<
zones u.	medium	mark.		o
m.	'' open.	rel. text		
l.	←	paraph		
size lets.		standard speed		
tapering	<	natural		
width in lets.		spacing		
bet. lets.		original.		
ind. lets.	K f	c - dom.		

Fig. 240

2

long forks and a purple, diamond-
shaped petrol tank. It also had one
of those two levelled seats where the
passenger sits slightly higher than the
rider. It looked really comfortable and
must have been going at about sixty.

This Thursday we're going to
the District Sports in Walton, the same
place as last year, though this time it
had better not pour with rain. Remember
last time when we got soaked to the
skin? This year I'm a reserve for
the relay team.

Nothing much has been happening at
school recently and its the exams in
a fortnights time so things are going
from bad to worse. Still, we've been
having plenty of days off recently — we've
been back from the last holiday five
weeks and we've had five days off
so far. We break up for the Summer
holidays three weeks after the exams although
of course you'll be back before then.

I hope you're having a good time in Spain,
I suppose it's scorching hot over there — we're
having lousy weather, as usual!

See you soon,

Richard.

Fig. 241

Fig. 241 shows the third side of a letter written by a fifteen-year-old English boy. Below is a step-by-step analysis of the letter:

1. A good standard of writing; it is legible with clear distances between the words and lines—he likes to be understood and has the ability to express himself clearly.

2. There are many left-direction tendencies. Most of the g and y endings are cut off on the leftward swing and all the endings on m and n curve backwards—not socially inclined.

3. Pressure is fairly heavy in the middle of words suggesting sudden outbursts of energy, both mental and physical. With the handwriting being well-formed a strong artistic sense is indicated.

4. The layout of the page is neat—good social background. Placed slightly to the right it points to an outward-looking attitude and a tendency to be impulsive. The irregular right margin shows a love of adventure and fluctuating social attitudes. The wide left margin indicates an element of shyness; its regularity suggests self-consciousness.

5. There are two larger gaps between words i.e. between 'This' and 'Thursday' (line 7), 'had' and 'five' (line 20) but since there are only two we can assume them to be hesitations while the writer wonders if it was Friday or Thursday and whether there were four days off or five. The spacing is generally well balanced; this indicates a certain lack of spontaneity but, at the same time, reveals a self-assured, unflappable personality. System, order and organization are important to him.

6. Taking into consideration the age of the writer we would expect the middle zone to be still fairly large. There is a left tendency in the middle zone indicating that emotions are suppressed. The length of projections fluctuate in both the upper and lower zones. The h in 'holiday' (line 22) is lower than the l and d and the two p's in 'suppose' (line 25) are stunted in relation to the g in the word beneath them.

Such fluctuations denote sensitivity, moods and a critical nature.

7. The size of the writing is average with plenty of variation in middle zone proportions—has the capacity to endure adversities.

8. The consistent horizontal line of writing emphasizes method and order; with the o's closed and the majority of a's we can deduce a straightforward, loyal and honest character.

9. The regularity of the writing shows great self-discipline and will-power and the ability to be a good, steady worker.

10. The garland connections predominate showing a kindly, sympathetic nature but there are many arcade forms, especially at the end of words, for example, 'team' (line 13) or 'been' (line 19) which imply an inhibitive factor—probably self-consciousness.

11. The degree of slant is between 100°–110° left, the area of reticence. Again taking the age into consideration, this left slant could represent sexual repression. A basic shyness dictates a preference for a small group of friends to whom the writer is extremely loyal but he is generally quite happy to be on his own.

12. As can be expected, the structure of the writing retains some of the roundness of an earlier childish form but many simplifications and a regular evenness reveal a clear, logical thought process and a conscientious, reliable attitude.

13. The breaks in words suggest a fund of imaginative and creative ideas.

14. The speed of writing is medium and regular—well-organized with a quick, decisive mental process.

15. There are no initial flourishes except on the letter f. He is direct and original; if he wants to do something he will do it and will do it well. All the final letters are well proportioned and clear—honest and reliable. The e endings, stopping short of an upward curve, indicate self-sufficiency

and a practical ability. He is very good at assessing people and is not easily deceived.

16. Some words expand: 'diamond' (line 1), 'where' (line 3), 'rain' (line 10), 'reserve' (line 12). Appearing in an intelligent handwriting expansion denotes a lack of diplomacy.

17. The left loop on f indicates that the past and mother are important to him. The cut-off loops of g and y emphasize his reticence and his desire for only a close circle of friends. However, the fact that some loops continue through and join to the next letter, as in 'slightly higher' (line 4), 'fortnights' (line 16), 'days' (line 20), show that he is perfectly capable of establishing other varied relationships. Compressed loops as in 'higher' (line 4), 'when' (line 11), indicate a reluctance to reveal his plans and ideas.

18. Little inward hooks appear on the last strokes of m and n, 'in' (line 8), 'when' (line 11), 'team' (line 13), 'happening' (line 14). The writer is capable of adopting a harsh, brusque attitude.

19. The signature is legible—sincerity. It is slightly larger than the text and the R has taken on a freer, more decorative form than any of the other capitals. He is asserting his independence and expressing an inner conviction that he will succeed in life: this is supported by the knot in the R which signifies thoroughness, and the short second downstroke of the R which reveals ambition. The dot following the signature is a decisive gesture of conclusion: he has nothing further to say and expects this to be understood. The absence of a paraph reveals an entirely natural personality.

20. Taking the individual letters, all the capital letters are in script—firm ego, high intelligence, cultured tastes. The capital I is a single downstroke emphasizing his characteristic straightforward, decisive approach to things. Many i dots are to the right of the stem—enthusiastic, observant, enquiring qualities; others are directly over the stem—order and method. The many open p's signify gentleness. The

small r finals, pointing straight ahead, are signs of energy
and enthusiasm. The capital T's, with the bars resting on
top of the stem, show that the writer thinks of the future;
the T in line 12 has the bar slightly above the stem and is
lighter in pressure—he is curious about things and prefers
to learn from experience. The small t bars are all either going
straight through the stem or emerging rightwards from the
stem; some are slightly pointing upwards. All are expressive of self-discipline and reliability.

FINAL ANALYSIS

Personality
The writer is highly intelligent, cultured and well co-
ordinated. His mental process is quick, clear and logical.
His totally straightforward nature will sometimes produce
tactlessness and even a brusque attitude but his general
manner is courteous. His remarkable self-discipline, will-
power and emotional control enable him to endure and
overcome adversities; he will keep calm in the face of chaos.

There are two equally forceful sides to his character:

1. a considered, methodical, practical approach to
matters where observation, organization and order are
important to him.

2. a spontaneous, energetic enthusiasm for adventure
where mental and physical energies will be vigorously
employed.

Social attitudes
He is not a socially inclined person. His self-assured bearing
cloaks a naturally shy and reticent nature. Self-consciousness and an inclination to be on the defensive create moods
and a tendency to be critical. He is clever at assessing people
and will rarely be taken in by them. His preference is for a
small group of close friends although his self-sufficient and
independent qualities allow him to be perfectly happy on

his own. His manner is direct; he is able to express himself well, keeps strictly to the point and knows when to stop. He will be reluctant to reveal more than he considers necessary.

He is basically gentle, kind and sympathetic but never sentimental. An underlying quick humour gives a healthy balance to his serious side.

41   Career Guidance

Career guidance is based on a person's interests and abilities.

Interests are formed by a combination of external influences (events, information, advice, encouragement) and internal influences (emotions, attitudes). External influences can be very powerful. They can persuade a person's inclinations towards a particular subject for which he may lack ability.

The graphologist must first discover what his client's interests are (hobbies, activities) and note which influences (external or internal) have been dominant in their formation. The handwriting must then be studied for evidence of mental and physical abilities.

MENTAL ABILITIES

Verbal comprehension	printed capital letters
Word fluency	open a and o; t bar joining to next letter; wide spacing
Numeracy	g and y like the figures 7 and 8; i dot carefully placed over stroke; no starting strokes.
Visual comprehension	wide left margin; circle i dot; good spacing

Memory	i dot carefully placed; careful punctuation; connected letters; thick t bar
Detail	exact dotting of i; careful punctuation
Logic	simplification; angular; right slant; connected letters; very small
Originality	original forms; disconnected letters; long t bar to right

PHYSICAL ABILITIES

Good health	fluid, quick, rhythmic writing with normal strong pressure; no breaks
Stamina	strong pressure
Energy	quick, regular, simplified writing; heavy pressure; i dot as dash to right
Physical activity	long swinging loops
Muscular co-ordination	heavy, firm, even pressure

Interests can now be compared with abilities and any interdependencies noted.

It is important to assess the client's values. Values represent the needs required for a career to sustain interest. By studying examples of handwriting covering a period of years the graphologist can trace the development of his client's values.

VALUES

Materialism	dominant lower zone with the lower loops having a broad triangular base; heavy pressure; heavy i dot

Altruism	right slant; letters having extending ends; stroke covering whole word
Prestige	right slant; large writing; initial letters of words larger than the rest; high capitals; endstrokes curving upwards to right
Responsibility	arcade strokes on capitals; regular; i dot carefully placed; closed a and o; t bar convex curve through stem; small capitals
Knowledge	small capitals; printed letters; good spacing
Aesthetics	wide left margin; small; upright; Greek E
Independence	high but simple capitals; arcade; upright; first stroke of capital M higher than the others

After comparing the dominant values with dominant interests and abilities it should be possible to assess which of the following career categories is most suitable for the client:

Constructive/Practical work	mechanics, building, etc.
Business	finance, publishing, etc.
Social	teaching, law, etc.
Creative	painting, literature, etc.
Interpretive	drama, exhibition work, etc.
Adaptive	design, editing, etc.
Scientific	mathematics, geology, etc.

The following is a list of qualities for careers and their corresponding graphological details:

accurate	carefully dotted i; small writing; angular
adaptable	g like an 8; m and n like w and u
aggressive	heavy t bar; right slant; long initial strokes
alert	light pressure
altruistic	right slant; stroke covering whole word; extending ends; endings of g and y turning to the right
ambitious	upward slope; right slant; the second downstroke of the capital R shortened; quick
argumentative	heavy t bar sloping downwards through stem, most letters disconnected; long initial strokes
artistic	wide left margin; wide spacing; arcade; pastose
business ability	wide spacing; right slant; words connected; angular
concentrate, ability to	small; simplified; narrow; no loops in lower zone; wide spacing; i dot carefully placed
constructive	printed capitals; small letters printed
conventions, respect for	copybook
co-ordination	good layout; good spacing; regular; large lower zone
creative	wide spacing; disconnected letters; wide script
critical mind	wide spacing; upright; large, even spacing between words
cultured	wide left margin; small d curving to left at top.
decisive	angular

determined	upward slope; thick t bar
diplomatic	arcade; words become narrower; illegible threads; a and o closed
disciplined, self	strong convex t bar through centre of stem
efficient	legible; clear distances between words and lines
emotions, flexible	round formations
energetic	fluid, quick, rhythmic writing; no breaks or amendments; simplified; i dots as dashes to right
enthusiastic	upward slope; t bar to right; i dot dash to right; upper zone more evident than lower
extravert	right slant; large writing
figures, talent for	g and y like 8 and 7
gentle	m and n have rounded tops
generous	right slant; long e finals
humorous	wavy t bar; curved i dots
ideas, talent for	un-uniform small letters
imaginative	high upper loops; end strokes with curl on end; t bar above stem
initiative	quick writing; disconnected
intuitive	disconnected in high standard writing
judgement, good	many closed a and o; always connected
kind	garlands; very light pressure
logical	connected; very small; right slant; angular; simplification
literary ability	Greek capital E; small d curving leftwards at top; y and g turning right
meditative	good spacing

memory, good	Connected; thick t bar; i dot low and directly over stem; careful punctuation; good word and line spacing
optimistic	upward slope
organize, ability to	good outlay and spacing; the upper and lower loops of the small f equally balanced
original	original letter forms; disconnected; high standard; pastose; long t bar right
pleasant nature	easy flow
people, ability to deal with	right slant
physical action, enjoys	long, swinging low loops
positive	upright and heavy
practical	wide, even spacing; e finals turned down; many closed small letters; steady line
quick-witted	no starting strokes, quick
reliable	regular; exact dotting of i; careful punctuation; garland; steady line; closed a and o; no left slant; small capitals; even, heavy pressure
shrewd	threads; upright
spiritual	large writing; dominant upper zone; light pressure
sympathetic	rounded formations; g and y endings to right; wide letters; narrow spacing
tactful	last letter smaller than rest; threads; closed a and o
teaching, love for	uniform formation
tenacious	upward hook on right of t bar; heavy pressure
thorough	heavy pressure; knots in f, t and k

42 Personnel Selection

As shown in the previous section, assessment of a person's abilities and values can be effectively compared graphologically with the qualities required for a particular job. In personnel selection the graphologist must also assess the applicant's working manner.

A person's abilities and values may be well suited to the demands of the job he has applied for but his working manner could be at variance with the normally accepted standards of the prospective employers.

Below is a list of graphological details and their corresponding conduct patterns:

Good speed; angular; regular, firm pressure; thick t bar; good spacing	A naturally hard worker; assertive and unflappable
A definite variety of pressure on downstrokes; slow speed	Fluctuating effort; will only do his best if he knows he is being watched; thrives on praise.
Stylized writing; embellished letter forms	Will always be trying to impress somebody
Words die out to threads in careless writing	Inconsiderate and slovenly
Right slant; heavy pressure; wavy t bar; curved i dot; good width; g like 8	Good-humoured; hard-working; co-operative
Every letter and word clearly written; firm t bars; careful punctuation; words increase in size; a and o closed	Honest
Upright; abrupt endings; a and o *always* closed	Quiet and reserved
Right slant; open capital D; many open a and o; words	Chatterbox

become larger towards endings	
Weak t bars	Lack of self-discipline; potential troublemaker
Large writing which tends to go in all directions; lack of spacing between lines; sporadic heavy downstrokes	Inattentive; unobservant; inconsiderate

43 Marriage Compatibility

The graphologist must be aware of the elements that combine to make a happy marriage. He must also be able to recognize, in analysis, discordant factors which could cause conflict within a marriage.

The introvert, reflective and extremely private, is no match for the extravert whose wholly outward-going nature is a constant source of aggravation to a sensitive person.

A left-slant handwriting (introvert) and a right-slant handwriting (extravert) will signify conflicting temperaments. Two right-slant handwritings will be compatible. Two left-slant handwritings will be compatible but they will need the binding quality of a mutual interest.

A person with a left-slant exceeding 130° should not marry.

An upright slant in light pressure will work with a left-slant; an upright slant in heavy pressure will work with a right-slant. (It must be remembered that an upright slant, 95°–85°, signifies restraint in all things).

Below is a list of essential mutual qualities for a happy marriage. The corresponding graphological details must be found in both handwritings:

Tolerance	the letter g resembles the figure 8; the letter y has a

	right stroke; open capital D, a and o
Co-operation	disconnected letters (high standard); g and y like 8 and 7
Self-control	convex t bar through stem
Sympathy	rounded formations
Humour	wavy t bar; curved i dots
Physical compatibility	a spirited, flowing writing with long rhythmic lower loops

44 Mental Aberrations and Handwriting

PSYCHOPATHIC PERSONALITY

An anti-social personality which is often the result of emotional deprivation or harsh chastisement in early childhood. It manifests itself in abnormally aggressive or lawless behaviour and among its many characteristics are superficial charm, unreliability, lack of remorse, poor judgement and sexual maladjustment.

In handwriting it can be detected by already written passages being covered with new words.

PARANOIA

An intricate, slowly developing, delusional state which is isolated from the rest of the personality leaving the intelligence unaffected. Delusions are often of a grandiose nature.

In handwriting paranoia can be detected by the heavy

underlining of *all* words, fragmentary handwriting, mounting lines, pictures instead of words, any very unusual or totally unintelligible writing or where whole sentences are joined by continuous connections of words without spacing.

HOMICIDAL MANIA

A condition of attempting or desiring to kill which is usually accompanied by melancholia and suicidal feelings.

The appearance of the handwriting is affected by frequent blocks of heavy pressure within normal pressure (Fig. 242).

SCHIZOPHRENIA

There are many forms of schizophrenia but the general manifestation of it is in a slowly progressive deterioration of the whole personality with the main characteristic of withdrawal from reality.

In handwriting the line directions chop and change—a permanent graphological characteristic (Fig. 243), letters are broken or split, often there is a sudden incongruity between very thin and very thick strokes (Fig. 244).

PSYCHO-NEUROTIC DEPRESSION

This condition is frequently precipitated by some current personal crisis which is often connected with guilt feelings. The acutely depressed state disappears with the removal of the cause.

It is reflected in handwriting by small, light, left-directed letters in a downward slope with weak connective strokes. Any signature is usually placed to the left.

HYPOCHONDRIASIS

A morbid concern with body functions and exaggeration of symptoms. The hypochondriac ignores the outer world and directs all his interest and energy to the part of his body which preoccupies him.

Revealed in handwriting by joined breaks (Fig. 245), laborious writing, duplication of letters or parts of letters (Fig. 246).

MANIA

A disorder characterized by an elated, unstable mood, agitation and an increase in speed of grandiose thoughts and speech.

Reflected in handwriting by an increasing extreme right slant which becomes almost horizontal (Fig. 247).

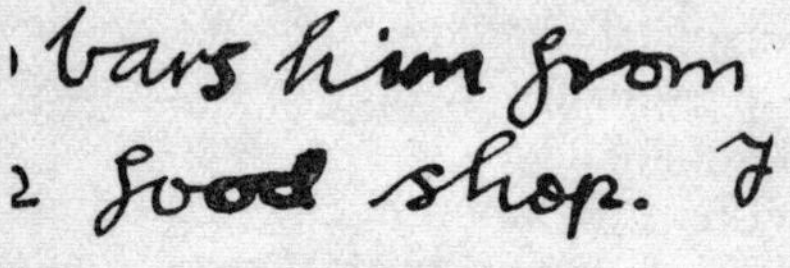

Fig. 242

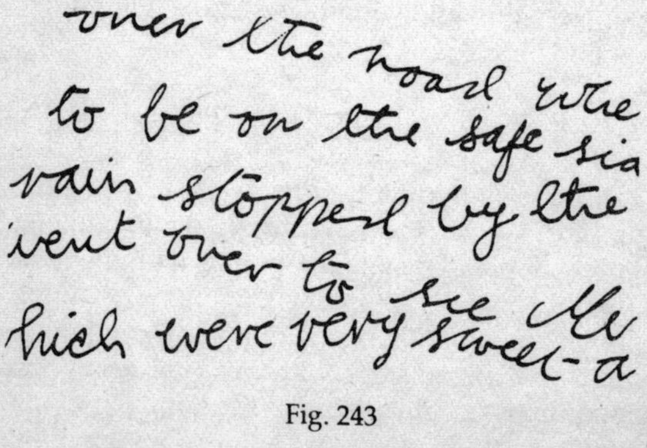

Fig. 243

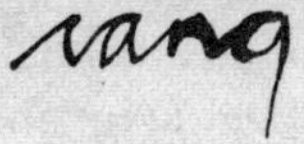

rang

Fig. 244

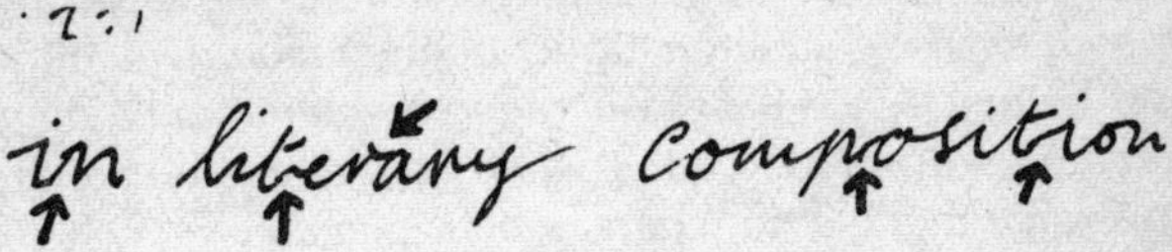

in literary composition

Fig. 245

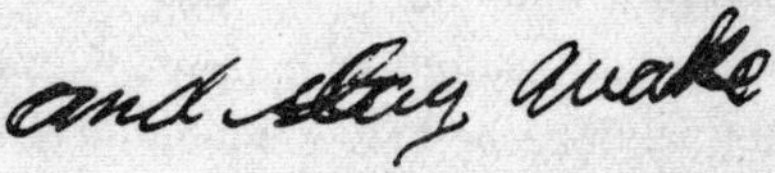

and stay awake

Fig. 246

Fig. 247

45 Forgery

The forger is likely to apply his attention to the obvious structures of a handwriting for example capital letters, downstrokes and letters with loops; he tends to ignore the middle zone, the slant of upstrokes within words, pressure and stroke endings.

Forgery requires great concentration and any form of concentration will induce strain and exhaustion as can be witnessed at the ends of forged words: having concentrated on the formation of the letters of a word the relief at reaching the final letter causes a lapse in attention and this makes the last letter of any word a main target for study. There will be no natural spontaneous flow of line but, instead, a wavering, weak effort. Other points to look for are t bars which are free, expressive strokes; the small a and o which can be characteristically open or closed; all middle zone letters, some of which can characteristically change direction within a word; i dots which, again, are free, expressive marks with characteristic placings over, behind or before the stem; spacing between words which is unconsciously expressed.

In a page of suspectedly forged writing the above points must be looked for plus line slope, spacing between lines and the width and uniformity of margins.

Nobody's writing is absolutely identical; in a word written over and over again by the same person (Fig. 248) many differentiations will be observed but the basic structure of the word is the same as is the spontaneous flow and the slight rise in line slope.

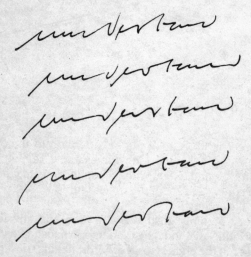

Fig. 248

Fig. 249a

Fig. 249b

Fig. 250

Figs. 249a and 249b show original signatures written by Colin Hadley. Fig. 250 is a forgery. The two original signatures show differentiations most noticeably in the c, o, H and d, but both have a spontaneous, natural flow. The forgery does not flow and lacks any sign of spontaneity. To illustrate some of the points to look for I will compare the forgery with the originals step by step:

1. Very noticeable is the slope differentiation: the two originals are rising but the forgery slopes downwards (place

a ruler on a horizontal line under the base of the capital C's).

2. In the originals the capital C's both start their bottom curves directly opposite the top curves; the back curves of the C's are fairly straight, pressure is light to medium. The forgery shows the back-curve to be erratic in pressure and form with the bottom curve beginning to the right of the opposite upper curve.

3. The o's have heavy pressure on their downward curves, light on their up-curves. The forgery is light all the way round.

4. The joining strokes between the o's and the l's are in medium pressure and firm. The forgery stroke is wavery and fluctuates in pressure.

5. In the two l's the downward strokes are heavy, relieving pressure on the following upswings. The forgery is vice versa.

6. The joins of the l's to the i's are sharply pointed. The forgery shows a thick point which is slightly rounded.

7. The same occurs with the i upsweeps to the n's—the join is sharp and pointed. The forgery is angled to the right.

8. In the two originals the first downstrokes of the n's are off-centre to the right. In the forgery the first downstroke is off-centre to the left.

9. The strokes from the base of the downstrokes to the tops of the second downstrokes are straight and culminate in a point. The corresponding stroke in the forgery is curved and culminates in a curve.

10. Now comes the final stroke of the first name. The two final downstrokes begin straight down with heavy pressure, curving lightly outwards to abrupt endings. The final downstroke in the forgery takes a right direction heavy downstroke continuing into a thick upward ending.

11. Having completed the first name the forger's relief is reflected in his careless attitude towards the i dot. In the two originals the i dots are in the form of a sideways v, the upper strokes extremely light, the lower strokes starting heavily and finishing lightly. Both are placed directly over the last

downstroke of the n. In the forgery only one mark is made, starting lightly and finishing heavily. It is placed mid-way over the joining loop from the i to the n.

12. Our forger is now very anxious to attack the second name and off he goes to make the first stroke of the H quite ignoring the very important distance between the two names. (Distances between words happen unconsciously and, in a good standard of handwriting, they present a major point in forgery detection). There is a differentiation of 1¼mm. between the two originals, the smaller distance being exactly 10mm. The distance between the two names in the forgery is 6mm.

13. In the originals the first downstrokes of the H's carry on upwards in a very faint line directing towards the top of the second downstrokes. If you take a ruler and place it on line with the faint upswings you will see that the lines connect with the curved hooks at the tops of the second downstrokes. Repeating this exercise with the forgery you will find that the line of the ruler misses the rounded hook by 1mm. The forger has noticed and put in the base upward hook and the top curved hook but has failed to realize that they form the beginning and end of a very faint connecting stroke.

14. While the H downstrokes in the originals are quick, straight strokes of even pressure, those of the forgery are tremulous and fluctuate in pressure.

15. The linking lines from the H's to the a's in the originals are firm, slight curves. The link in the forgery is wavering and boomerang-shaped.

16. The connecting lines from the a's to the d's, and including the whole of the d's, are made in one flowing stroke of medium to light pressure. That of the forgery begins with a heavy, short, downward stroke from the a, curving and rising to the d where heavy pressure and wavering lines reveal hesitation and careful drawing.

17. The tops of both d's in the originals rise up and curve over with light pressure. That of the forgery curves slightly

leftwards and finishes with a heavy dot.

18. The 'ley's' of the originals form three flowing garland curves in medium pressure. The garlands of the forgery in 'ley' fluctuate in pressure, do not form evenly flowing curves and there is a hesitation in the upcurve from the 1.

19. Now the forger comes to the last letter of the second name and here the tension is obvious. In the originals the y's are made with one stroke; they descend 13mm. and immediately rise to the right in a firm, curving, vanishing line. The forged y, although written in one stroke, is tremulous, fluctuating in pressure, descends 16½mm., forms a blob at the turning point and ends with an irregular curve which does not vanish but terminates with a small dot.

Conclusive and sufficient evidence of forgery is produced by the findings in paragraphs 1, 2, 8, 11, 12, 13, 17, 18, 19.

46   Disguised Handwriting

Fig. 251 shows the natural writing of a young man. Fig. 252 shows disguised writing by the same person. In this case, the young man is not forging a handwriting; he is merely changing his own manner of writing in the hope that, for some reason, it will not be detected as his. A step-by-step comparison follows to show how the young man can be revealed as being the writer of both examples.

u not be used towards the purchase.

Fig. 251

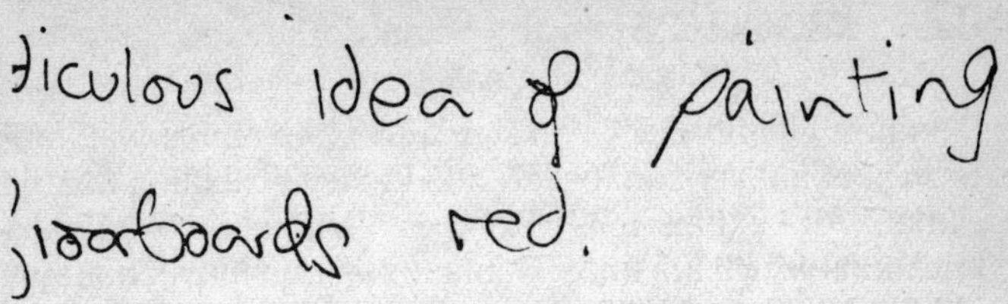

ticulous idea of painting

floorboards red.

Fig. 252

Firstly, spacing. The spacing between words in both writings is an almost regular 10mm.

Secondly, slant. The slant of the t stems in Fig. 251 are both 105° left as is the t in 'painting' in Fig. 252.

Thirdly, the t bars all begin just to the left of the stem.

In the absence of i dots in Fig. 251, the above three points are the most important to look for.

The conspicuous letters, d, f, p, g, b, are ignored for it is in the middle zone that concentration wavers. Thus we find that the first u in 'ridiculous' is identical to that in 'used'; the s's in 'towards', 'purchase', 'ridiculous' and 'floorboards' all curve down to a point from which a short, straight stroke turns leftwards. In 'towards' the o meets at the top from where a rightward line joins it to the following letter. The same sequence occurs in 'ridiculous'. Also in 'towards' the formation of the connecting a and r is repeated in 'floorboards'. The final curve of the e in 'used' stops short just before the curve of the following d. Although the word 'red' is in lighter pressure the relation of the e ending to the d curve is identical to that in 'used'.

Apart from the above similarities, the tremulously constructed n, the self-conscious g curve in 'painting' and the sudden heavy pressure, diminution of letter size and relatively cramped formation of 'loor' in 'floorboards' all point to a not entirely natural handwriting.

47 Doodles

Doodles, like flourishes on signatures, are regressive; they represent a reversion to childhood when scribbling was an outlet for expression. Doodles symbolize repressed emotions which are unconsciously released by internal and external associative influences and can only be successfully interpreted if those influences are made known.

Below is a list of some of the more usual shapes made in doodles with their meanings and notes of details to look for, where appropriate. The knowledge of slants, pressure, speed, placement and spacing, used in handwriting analysis can be applied equally to doodles.

Aeroplane	1. phallic symbol (probably more than one aeroplane; quickly drawn with light pressure)
	2. desire to escape monotony. (one aeroplane; a slow, detailed drawing in heavy pressure)
Arc	1. emotional feelings (concave; heavy pressure)
	2. uncertainty (convex or vertical, leaning left or right; slow with light pressure)
Arrow	1. symbol of the male sexual energy (more than one; quickly drawn)
	2. cruel feelings (slow with heavy pressure and thickening strokes)
	3. introversion (if penetrating something)
Bell	conscience (watch pressure for depth of feeling)
Circle	1. order, completeness, independence

(geometric circle perfectly joined;
firm pressure)

2. symbolic of female breasts;
mother influence

(flowing line, not joining but ends curling over)

3. anxiety and seclusion
(slow, hesitant line joined with
amendments; heavy pressure)

4. linked circles reflecting a logical
sequence
(quick; firm; small; moving to the
right)

Clouds   desire to escape
(light pressure)

Crown   self-confidence
(watch pressure for degree of
assurance)

Dots   concentration
(watch pressure and spacing)

Eye
1. symbolic of female genitals
(light pressure on outer curves,
heavier on pupil)

2. need for order and protection
(geometric; heavy)

Fence
1. inhibition
(round stockade formation)

2. self-control
(geometric; firm)

Fish   realistic approach to matters
(pressure will reveal depth of
interest)

Flower
1. circular: symbolic of womb
(one flower with inked-in centre)

2. phallic symbol
(more than one flower, some
with dropping petals; quickly
drawn)

Frame	1. caution (light, hesitant line with no gaps)
	2. with well-constructed doodle inside: orderly, systematic (quick, firm strokes; good layout)
	3. with poorly-constructed doodle inside: desires protection and security (weak, light pressure)
Lines—Parallel	1. mechanical existence (firm, horizontal, evenly spaced)
	2. reflection (vertical, light pressure; closely spaced)
	3. weak will (light pressure; sloping downwards)
Angular	aggression, hostility, resentment (heavy pressure)
Crossed	1. conflict (heavy pressure)
	2. a feeling of restriction (lines close together; heavy pressure; slow)
	3. an unconscious desire to keep impulses under control (geometric: light pressure)
Complicated line patterns	defence against provocation
Short strokes (marks, dashes)	1. emotional confusion (light pressure; aimlessly drawn)
	2. restless energy force (heavy pressure; controlled disarray)
Square	1. trapped feeling (quickly and loosely drawn)

	2. materialistic (heavy pressure)
	3. practical (geometric construction of squares; firm pressure).
Steps	1. sexually symbolic (quick; heavy pressure)
	2. ambition (slow; firm)
Snake	1. phallic symbol: passion (curving; flowing)
	2. enlightenment, understanding (curving around an upright)
Star	1. five points: harmonious
	2. six points: objective
Tick	concentration (watch pressure)
Trees	1. one tree: phallic symbol
	2. more than one: developing thoughts
Triangle	1. symbolic of male genitals
	2. strong-minded (heavy pressure; firm)
Web	1. self-preoccupation (intricate design; light pressure)
	2. anxiety (basic shape of inner strokes without the curving links; heavy, thick strokes)
Wheel	dynamic urge
Whorl	1. clockwise: mentally alert (heavy pressure)
	2. anti-clockwise: regression (light pressure)
	3. tightly drawn: tension
	4. loosely drawn: relaxation

48 List of Qualities, Deficiencies, Physical and Mental Form with Graphological Details

(additional words can be found listed in Section 41)

abrupt	abrupt finals
absent-minded	no t bar; no i dot
adventurous	irregular right slant
aesthetic	wide/very wide left margin; small letters; Greek E.
affected	overlarge interspaces
affectionate	right slant; wide letters
agreeable	wide even loops; well-shaped garlands
aloof	upright
amoral	counterstrokes
animated	t bars to right; i dots to right; hasty
anti-social	all letters disconnected
anxious	retracing of words; words set too closely together; narrow letters; jamming letters in words.
ardent	heavy pressure
arrogant	capital M with strokes decreasing; upright; high capitals
articulate	writing line fluent
athletic	long lower loops; heavy pressure
attention, desire for	red ink; initial letters larger than others
autocratic	signature larger than writing
automatic	legible but lacking originality
avaricious	upright; narrow letters
balanced	regular and rhythmic writing
bashful	small letters; low capitals and

	loops; e finals weak and descend to the right
bluff	counterstrokes
boastful	large capitals; counterstrokes
bold	heavy pressure; large letters; wide spacing
bossy	large, broad t bars on top of stems; g loop triangle
brave	heavy pressure; e finals ascend to right
brilliant	small, angular writing
brusque	large letters; heavy pressure; high capitals; heavy descent of e final to right
brutal	heavy pressure; t bar thicker at final; e finals thick; slow writing with left slant and not very clear letters
busybody	elaboration of capitals and initial letters of words; superfluous strokes
calm	upright, fine, even writing
careless	missing t bar; missing i dot
cautious	initial letters detached from rest of the word; closed a and o; upright; t bar left of stem; i dot left of stem
charming	upright
clean	good spacing
clever	crossing two t stems with one bar which flows into the next letter
comprehension, high degree of	constant right margin with no split words or compressed words
conceit	high capitals; overlarge inter-spaces
concentration	small writing; simplified; no loops in lower zone; wide

	spacing; i dot low and directly over stem
concentration, lack of	tall, wide, right slanting writing in light pressure
conscientious	small, even writing; i dot low and directly over stem
considerate	good spacing; letters of uniform height
co-operative (unco-operative)	right slant; g and y like 8 and 7; wide writing low standard, disconnected writing
cowardice	light pressure; e finals weakly descending to right; weak t bar
cumbersome	elaboration of capitals and initial letters of words; superfluous strokes
cunning	letters confused; threads; a and o tightly knotted; heavy pressure
daring	4mm. or more
deceitful	threads; letters varying in size; a and o tightly knotted; pressure comes in lumps
demonstrative (undemonstrative)	right slant extreme left slant
dependable	stable line; upright; a and o closed
depression	small writing; weak or too heavy pressure; descending lines
detached	extreme left slant
diligent	large starting strokes; heavy, right slant
discipline, lack of	light pressure and over-large letters
discouraged, easily	extremely light pressure
dishonest	letters varying in size; broken garland stroke in a, o and d
distrustful	narrow writing; covering strokes
dreamer	top loop of initial letter inflated;

	addresses envelopes in top left corner
economic	narrow left margin; simplification
educated	simplification; speed; printed letters; ends of words decrease
emotional delusions	concealed letters in middle zone
emotional instability	gross fluctuation of letter size; irregular word spacing; varying pressure
emotional flexibility	round formations
enterprise	quick, large, broad writing; long initial stroke above letter
erotic	pictorial letters; upper zone into lower zone of line above
exaggeration	very large writing; very large lower loops
excitable	heavy pressure; t bar upwards; initial letters have a long, rising stroke; variation in slant
extravagant	widening left margin; few words in a large space
fashionable	neat writing with tasteful embellishments; violet ink
fastidious	small writing; punctuation carefully placed
fatigue	upper loops occasionally broken or tremulous
firm	medium/heavy pressure; thick t bar
frank	stable base line; a and o mostly open; expanding words
friendly	garland; right slant; gentle, even loops in lower zone
fussy	small writing; dash i dots; punctuation carefully placed
genuine	speed; simplification

gregarious	narrow right margin; right slant
gullible	low loops on l and t
hasty	widening margin; t bars right and long; narrow right margin
headstrong	heavy pressure; tall capitals; strong and full-length downstrokes
health, good	fluid, quick writing; medium/strong pressure; no breaks or amendments
health, bad	weak or very heavy pressure; slow, small writing of a generally low standard; breaks and tremulous strokes; many amendments
hearty	right slant; wide writing
helpful	good symmetry
highly strung	4mm. or more
honest	expanding words; speed; simplification; high standard; right slant; a and o closed; fully legible
humility	small capitals
hypocrisy	a, o, d and b open at base; pressure in lumps
hysteria	thread inside words
idealist	large writing; dominant upper zone; right slant
imagination, lack of	copybook; low loops
immaturity	small m with round tops; t bar before stem
impatient	tall letters; light pressure; right slant
impractical	no margins with writing around the edges
impress, desire to	elaboration of capitals; elaborate initial letters; superfluous strokes
impressionable	upper loops sometimes tall, sometimes short

impudent	low standard
impulsive	left margin widening; letters nearly always disconnected; t bars right and long; up-slope
inconsiderate	illegible
inconsistent	uneven left margin
independent	upright; stable line; first stroke of capital M higher than others; e finals very long; thick t bar; high but simple capitals
indolent	arcade in slow writing
industrious	symmetry
inferiority	illegible; amendments
inhibition	small writing; heavy pressure slow
insecure	retouching
insincere	arcade
inspiration	breaking up of words
intellectual	simplification; no starting strokes
intelligent	good layout; clear spacing; simplification; words diminishing; connection of t bar or i dot with previous or following letter
intolerant	narrow left margin or none at all; angular; narrow writing
introvert	left slant
irrational	disintegrating letters
irresponsible	concave t bar
irritable	very high t bar; dash i dots; hasty; frequent omissions
jealousy	consistent exaggeration of a or o inside words; very right slant; finals strong and descend to the right; large writing expanding to huge
jolly	large, flowing writing; rising finals; wavy t bars; curved i dots

judgement, good	upright; small, connected writing; g and y like 8 and 7; a and o closed
justice, strong sense of	right with heavy pressure
lazy	slow, upright writing; neglected formations with arcades
leadership	large, regular writing with heavy pressure
level-headed	upright
liar	arcade; concealing strokes; slow; left
literary tastes	large, even spacing between words; g like 8
lonely	every available space used
loner	downstrokes culminating in tight circles
loyal	stable base line; closed a and o
lucid	legibility; clear distances between words and lines
materialistic	dominant lower zone; heavy i dot; baseline below printed line; broad triangular base on lower loops
megalomania	over-large writing
memory, lack of	large break inside words; the leaving out of letters and words
meticulous	angular
mind, business	good general outlay; good spacing
mind, clear	good spacing
mind, narrow	narrow left margins or none at all; e finals descend
mind, scientific	simplification; connecting t bar or i dot with preceding or following letter; small
miserly	small, compressed writing; t bar with upturning hook

modesty	small writing with small capitals
moody	irregular writing on a wavy baseline; left margin uneven and untidy; variation in slant
musical	very wide, rounded upper loop; pictorial notes
neat	control of left and right margins; organised pattern
nerves, bad	tremulous features; irregular
neurotic	neglect of form and confusion of letters; compulsive corrections; bad spatial arrangement
numeracy	quick; no starting strokes; carefully placed i dot
objective	very small writing
observant	tent i dot; disconnected; very small writing; angular
obstinate	abrupt finals; heavy pressure; heavy t bar slanting downwards
obtrusive	small spacing between words; small margins; lower and upper zones mixing; no paragraphs
patient	slow writing; m and n have angular tops
peace-loving	slow writing of good standard with some arcades
pedantic	continuous joining of words with short threads
perceptive, keenly	angular
perfectionist	high upper loops
perseverance	knotted t bar; heavy pressure
persistence	heavy pressure
pessimistic	upright (90°–95°); addresses envelopes near the bottom
physical type	pastose
physical, weak	rounded handwriting with no t bars; descending lines

physical, strong	heavy pressure
pliable	childish handwriting
poetic tastes	curled endings on e, w, and d
poise	upright
possessive	horizontal finals in heavy pressure; up-hook on t bars
precision	low, direct i dot
pride	wide left margin, small capitals
procrastination	first letter stands apart; t bar left of stem; i dot left of stem
protective	t bar covering a whole word; stroke on finals curving back over the top of the last letter
purposeful	finals ending in points
quarrelsome	long, rising initial strokes; rising t bar; heavy pressure; dash i dots
quiet	light pressure
reader	printed letters
realist	dominant lower zone; disconnected writing; upright
reasonable	connected
rebellious	capital I starting from the baseline
reckless	right slant 50°
religious	dominant upper zone; finals rising to upper zone; high, large capitals
repressed	vertical, angular writing in heavy pressure
resentful	small, narrow, angular writing
reserved	large distance between words; upright or left slant; a and o always closed; fairly narrow writing
revengeful	top and bottom loops pointed
ruthless	very narrow writing
sadistic	upright writing with heavy

	pressure; finals very heavy and pointing downwards; flooded middle zone and loops
sarcastic	wavy t bar; tent i dot; lancelike downstrokes
secretive	concealing strokes; a and o always closed; capital letter hides second letter; wide margins all around
self-admiring	the right stroke of the capital L extending under the word
self-centred	very narrow writing
self-confident	large, quick, uniform writing in heavy pressure; thick t bar; little or no space between words
self-conscious	control of left and right margins; narrow writing
self-devaluation	small i for capital I
self-dramatising	first letter of words disproportionately high
self-protecting	claw strokes in lower zone
selfish	e finals absent or curling under word
sensitive	wide loops; extremely light pressure
sentimental	compresses words and lines at bottom of page; right slant; excessive underscoring and use of punctuation
sex drive	strong lower zone
sex excitement	mingling of upper and lower loops
sex fantasy	thread loops
sex, fear of	neglected lower zone
sex frustration	loop irregularities
sex guilt	capital I slants left in upright or right slant writing

sex inhibition	heavy on downstrokes only
sex, rejection of	no loops in lower zone
shy	narrow capitals; wide left margin; diminishing right margin
sincere	words increase in size; closed a and o; no left slant; stable line; right slant; legible signature
sociable	dominant middle zone; right extension of end strokes; large writing; capital M has pointed tops
softly spoken	light pressure; light t bars
spatial ability	quick writing; no starting strokes; i dot direct
speaker, good	writing legible with clear spacing between words and lines
spontaneous	speed; simplification
stable	uniform writing
stubborn	e finals strong and descend to right; heavy t bar slants downwards
subjective	4mm. or more
subordination	small writing; low t bars
suicidal	small, disconnected writing with weak or heavy pressure; no starting strokes; large spacing; downward slope; pictorial; signature to left
superiority, feeling of	decreasing words from small to very small; high, large capitals
superiority complex	8–12mm.
suspicious	decreasing right margin; variation in slant; heavy horizontal finals
systematic	connected writing
taciturn	concealed middle zone
talented	printed letters, especially s

talkative	no margins; open a and o; broad writing
temper	e finals strong and descend to right; heavy t bars
thrifty	no margins; compressed writing
timewaster	elaborate initial letter
timid	e finals weak and descend to right; light pressure
tired	small writing with low pressure and descending line; no t bar
touchy	enlarged a or o inside words; light pressure
tough	knots in f, t, k
trustworthy	clear writing with well-proportioned final letters
truthful	stable line; a and o closed
two-faced	tall, wide letters; light pressure; left slant
uncouth	variation in size of letters; untidy, ill-formed
unflappable	good spacing of words and lines
unreliable	t bar left of stem and pointing downwards; convex line slope with heavy pressure diminishing to light pressure; illegible signature
unsophisticated	slow writing with arcades
untidy	thread finals
vacillation	last letter stands apart
vain	high capitals with inflated B, P, D
versatile	variation in t bars; use of Greek E and printed E; unconnected and connected writing
violent	pictorial; heavy downward finals
vitality	quick, fluid, rhythmic, simplified writing; no breaks or amendments; medium/strong pressure

warm personality	right slant
weak-willed	weak t bar
word fluency	wide spacing; long t bar to right; t bar joining following letter
worried	line slopes downwards; dash i dots.

Recommended Bibliography

CREPIEUX-JAMIN, J. *Handwriting and Expression* London, 1892

CREPIEUX-JAMIN, J. *The Psychology of the Movements of Handwriting* London, 1926

JACOBY, HANS *Analysis of Handwriting* New York, 1940

KLAGES, LUDWIG *Die Probleme der Graphologie* Leipzig, 1910

KLAGES, LUDWIG *Handschrift und Charakter* Leipzig, 1940

LANGENBRUCH, WILHELM *Praktische Menschenkenntnis auf Grund der Handschrift* Berlin, 1929

MICHON, J. *Systeme de Graphologie* Paris, 1875

MICHON, J. *La Method Practique de Graphologie* Paris, 1878

PULVER, MAX *Trieb und Verbrechen in der Handschrift* Zurich, 1934

PULVER, MAX *Symbolik der Handschrift* Zurich, 1940

PULVER, MAX *Intelligenz im Schriftausdruck* Zurich, 1949

ROMAN, KLARA *Handwriting: A Key to Personality* London, 1954

SAUDEK, ROBERT *The Psychology of Handwriting* London, 1925

SAUDEK, ROBERT *Experiments with Handwriting* New York, 1929

VICTOR, F. *The Copybook Forms of 15 Nations* Berlin, 1930

VICTOR, F. *Handwriting: A Personality Projection* Springfield, 1952